George Thistlethwaite

Über die Sprache in Tennyson's Idylls of the King

In ihrem Verhältniss zur Bibel und zu Shakspere

George Thistlethwaite

Über die Sprache in Tennyson's Idylls of the King
In ihrem Verhältniss zur Bibel und zu Shakspere

ISBN/EAN: 9783743488069

Hergestellt in Europa, USA, Kanada, Australien, Japan

Cover: Foto ©Thomas Meinert / pixelio.de

Manufactured and distributed by brebook publishing software
(www.brebook.com)

George Thistlethwaite

Über die Sprache in Tennyson's Idylls of the King

UEBER DIE SPRACHE
IN TENNYSON'S IDYLLS OF THE KING
IN IHREM VERHÄLTNISS
ZUR BIBEL UND ZU SHAKSPERE.

INAUGURAL-DISSERTATION

ZUR

ERLANGUNG DER DOCTORWÜRDE

DER

HOHEN PHILOSOPHISCHEN FACULTÄT

DER

VEREINIGTEN FRIEDRICHS-UNIVERSITAT

HALLE-WITTENBERG

VORGELEGT VON

GEO. THISTLETHWAITE

AUS ENGLAND.

HALLE A. S.
HOFBUCHDRUCKEREI VON C. A. KAEMMERER & CO.
1896.

TO MY FRIEND

WARD GRANVILLE.

Einleitung.

Die Dichtungen A. Tennysons zeigen bei aller Originalität doch in Inhalt und Form so unverkennbare Beziehungen zu früheren Werken der englischen Litteratur, dass sie der litterarhistorischen Forschung ein weites Gebiet der Thätigkeit eröffnen. Es lassen sich sowohl Beeinflussungen als auch direkte Nachahmungen aufzeigen, und zwar gilt dies für keins seiner Werke in so hohem Masse wie gerade für die hervorragendste Schöpfung seines dichterischen Genius, die Idylls of the King. Es ist dies ein Epencyklus, an dem der Dichter ein halbes Jahrhundert hindurch gearbeitet hat und der dennoch ein grossartiges einheitliches Ganze bildet, eine dichterische Verkörperung seiner ethischen und religiösen Weltanschauung. Ich gebe zunächst über diese Idylls einige allgemein orientierende Bemerkungen.

Das ganze Werk besteht aus 12 Einzelgesängen, veröffentlicht in der Zeit von 1842 bis 1885, aber nicht etwa in chronologischer Reihenfolge; er begann vielmehr mit dem Schluss, der Morte d'Arthur, die er 1842 herausgab, aber, wie sich nachweisen lässt, schon geraume Zeit vorher geplant hatte. Siebzehn Jahre vergingen, bis weiteres erschien: erst 1859 gelangten "Enid", "Vivien", "Elaine" und „Guinevere" zur Veröffentlichung. Zehn Jahre später, 1869, gab der Dichter "The Coming of Arthur", "The Holy Grail", "Pelleas and Ettarre" und "The Passing of Arthur" heraus, welch letzteres die Morte d'Arthur von 1842 mit enthielt. Dann folgte "The Last Tournament" 1871, "Gareth and Lynette" 1872, und schliesslich 1885 "Balin and Balan", womit die Reihe vollständig wurde. Die gegenwärtige Gruppierung der Gedichte ist folgende: "The Coming of Arthur" bildet die Einleitung, "The Passing of Arthur" den Schluss, die übrigen zehn Idylle, die unter der Ueberschrift "The Round Table", zusammengefasst sind, stehen in der Mitte. Wir sehen also, dass Tennyson mit dem Ende begann, dann den Anfang dichtete, und mit der Mitte aufhörte. Obgleich jedoch die "Idylls" zu verschiedenen Zeiten und in unregelmässiger Folge geschrieben wurden, bilden sie doch in ihrer endgültigen Anordnung ein harmonisches Ganze mit regelrechter Entwickelung und einheitlichem Plan. Die erzählten Begebenheiten füllen einen Zeitraum von einem Jahre aus, und die verschiedenen Erscheinungsformen der Natur vom Anfang bis zum Ende des Jahres bezeichnen zugleich die einzelnen Stufen der allmählig, aber unaufhaltsam fortschreitenden Entwickelung der einen grossen Schuld, die anfangs unscheinbar aufkeimend immer mehr und mehr Gebiet gewinnt, um schliesslich das ganze Reich zu umstricken und König Arthur und seine Tafelrunde dem Untergange preiszugeben.

"The Coming of Arthur" berichtet von der geheimnissvollen Geburt Arthurs in der Neujahrsnacht, von seiner Vermählung, von der Gründung der Tafelrunde und seines Reiches, von seinem Kampfe gegen Rom und von der Besiegung der „heidnischen Horden in zwölf grossen Schlachten". — Den Höhepunkt ihres Ruhmes hat Arthurs Herrschaft erreicht in "Gareth and Lynnette". Gareth verlässt die Heimat, um an den Hof zu gehen, zu der Jahreszeit, wo die Vögel ertönen lassen "melody on branch.... for it was past the time of Easterday". Das Feuer der Jugend, dass in ihm lodert, muss sich nach aussen bethätigen. Er brennt vor Begierde, Proben seines Mutes abzulegen, aber er will seine Tapferkeit allein in den Dienst der Ehre, der Tugend und der Wahrheit stellen,

zu deren Förderung die Tafelrunde gegründet war. In
hochherziger Begeisterung unternimmt er die Befreiung der
Gefangenen aus dem "Castle Perilous", die seiner Be-
harrlichkeit und Unerschrockenheit auch wirklich gelingt.
Damit hat er sich als echten Ritter bewährt, dessen höchste
Aufgabe ist: Kampf gegen Unrecht und Gewaltthat in jeder
Gestalt. Es ist jetzt noch die Zeit der Reinheit und Un-
schuld, die Zeit, wo „every chance brought out a
noble knight", und wo die Menschen "live pure, speak
true, and right wrong". — In "The Marriage of
Geraint" und "Geraint and Enid", zwei Idyllen, von
denen das zweite die Fortsetzung des ersten bildet, hat die
Zeit einen Schritt vorwärts gethan, denn die Erzählung
setzt ein, „on a summer morn". Jetzt hören wir zum
ersten Male von der Sünde, die schliesslich den Untergang
des Reiches herbeiführt, "when a rumour rose about the
Queen, touching her guilty love for Lancelot". Aus Furcht,
dass Enid verführt werden könnte, nimmt Geraint sie vom
Hofe weg. — Die Kunde von der Schuld der Königin dringt
in "Balin and Balan" über den Kreis des Hofes hinaus
und verbreitet sich immer weiter und weiter in "Merlin
and Vivien", wo am Schluss ein Sommergewitter ge-
schildert wird. In "Lancelot and Elaine" ist es noch "full
Summer". Hier haben wir bereits eine Frucht der Sünde;
denn an Elaine's Tod ist die Kunde von der unerlaubten
Liebe Lancelots zu Guinevere schuld. — In "the Holy
Grail" fangen die Ritter an, ihre Pflicht zu versäumen, und
jagen während der Abwesenheit ihres Herrn "wandering
fires" nach. "Pelleas and Ettarre" is das letzte der
Sommeridylle, und während der Sommer zu Ende geht,
schwindet gleichzeitig Ehre, Wahrheit und Tugend dahin;
denn Ettarre scheut sich nicht sich offen mit einem Manne
zu vergehen, den sie eben erst kennen gelernt hat. Der
Herbst mit seinem "yellowing leaf" folgt in "the Last
Tournament": die Tafelrunde mit ihren Gelübden wird offen
verspottet. Die Zeit, in der die Handlung von "Guinevere"

spielt, ist der Beginn des Winters. Die Königin flieht in ein Kloster, die Sünde des Hofes ist dem Lande bekannt geworden, die Tafelrunde löst sich auf, das Reich geht zu Grunde, und Arthur geht seinem Schicksal entgegen. "The Passing of Arthur", dessen Schluss ebenso düster als ergreifend ist, versetzt uns in die Jahreszeit, wo "the great light of heaven, burned at his lowest in the rolling year". Der König, der in der letzten "weird battle" im Westen den Verräter Modred besiegt hat, verlässt, ohne dass die Reinheit seines Charakters und seiner Ehre je durch einen Flecken getrübt worden ist, diese Welt so geheimnisvoll, als er in sie eingetreten ist. Ein Boot entführt ihn, wie er es vorausgesagt hatte.

Jedes dieser Idylle giebt eine in sich abgeschlossene Einzelhandlung, bildet aber zugleich auch ein Glied einer Kette. Jedes hat seinen bestimmten Platz in einer Reihe, als deren Mittelpunkt Arthurs überragende Gestalt erscheint. Und doch ist das Ganze nicht ein Epos im gewöhnlichen Sinne des Wortes; zwar Anlage und Ton des Gedichtes ist episch, doch kommt zu diesem epischen Grundcharakter eine moralische Tendenz. Der Dichter spricht dies als seinen leitenden Gesichtspunkt selbst aus in seinem Epilog, in dem er das Werk bezeichnet als "a tale shadowing Sense ᷈t war with Soul". Andererseits sind die Personen aber auch nicht etwa blosse Vertreter von abstrakten Ideen; sie sind vielmehr wirkliche Menschen mit menschlichen Leidenschaften, Verirrungen und Schwächen.

In der eben genannten Schlussrede, die an die Königin Victoria gerichtet ist, macht Tennyson auch zwei seiner Quellen namhaft, wenn er Ihre Majestät bittet, dass sie anzunehmen geruhe,

"this old imperfect tale,
New-old, and shadowing Sense at war with Soul
Rather than that gray king, whose.name . . . .
. . . . or him
Of Geoffrey's book, or him of Malleor's".

Der Geoffrey, auf den hier hingewiesen wird, ist Gottfried von Monmouth, der Verfasser der Historia Britonum, deren Abfassungszeit zwischen die Jahre 1130 und 1147 fällt. Malleor ist Sir Thomas Malory, der die "Morte d'Arthur" schrieb, eine 1485 erschienene Sammlung von Romanen, die auf französische Quellen zurückgehen. Diese "Morte d'Arthur" Malorys hat Tennyson einigen seiner Idylle zu Grunde gelegt. Für eins derselben, "Geraint and Enid", entlehnte er den Stoff an dem Mabinogion, einer Sammlung von wallisischen Erzählungen.

Was Schönheit des Rhythmus, Erhabenheit des Tones, malerische Anschaulichkeit der Schilderung und Reichtum der Phantasie anbetrifft, so dürften die Idylle schwerlich ihres gleichen finden. Gleichwohl zeichnet sich die Sprache derselben durch eine Schlichtheit aus, die Tennyson zum Dichter des Volkes gemacht hat. Seit Shakspere's, ja man darf vielleicht sagen seit Chaucer's Zeiten hat wohl kein Schriftsteller Wörter romanischen Ursprungs mehr zu vermeiden gewusst als Tennyson. Man kann sagen, dass er sich am besten von allen englischen Dichtern auf das Malerische versteht. Seine Schilderungen zeigen in der Ausführung des Details eine Vollständigkeit, die von keinem Dichter übertroffen worden ist. Er versteht es, dem Leser Dinge und Personen mit glücklicher Realistik lebendig vor Augen zu führen.

Wie Milton im "Verlorenen Paradies" so hat Tennyson in den Idyllen den 'blank verse' gebraucht, und mit einer Meisterschaft gehandhabt, wie sie seit Milton niemand erreicht hat. Wenn Miltons Verse eine stärkere Markierung des Taktes und grössere Klangfülle zeigen, so herrscht in denen Tennysons ein sanfter Ton, der ihm allein eigen ist.

In den Idyllen begegnen wir ausserordentlich oft der Allitteration in kunstvoller, feinsinniger Anwendung. Hierin war offenbar Spencer das Vorbild unseres Dichters. Auch in dem Sprachschatz, den Tennyson verwendet, bemerken

wir wie in dem Spensers viele Wörter, die dem älteren
Englisch angehören. Er folgt Spenser z B. in dem Gebrauch von Wörtern wie "ruth, wreak, trenchant, clomb",
und von Verbalformen wie "vext, snatcht, gript" etc. Auch
von Malory hat unser Dichter Wörter entlehnt, z. B,
"brewis, worshipful (im Sinne von honourable), avail" etc.
Einige Ausdrücke indessen hat er ganz allein, ohne dass
Entlehnung für dieselben nachweisbar wäre, z. B. "discaged,
increscent, decrescent" etc. Wir kommen auf diese Fälle
später zurück. Eine andere Eigentümlichkeit ist der häufige
Gebrauch kunstvoller Wiederholung, die wir am Schluss
belegen werden.

Der Gegenstand dieser Abhandlung ist die **Sprache**
der Idylls, und zwar in ihrer Abhängigkeit von der Sprache
der Vorgänger Tennysons.

Jedem, der mit der englischen Sprache und Litteratur
vertraut ist, muss der biblische Ton der Idylls auffallen,
sowie die Thatsache, dass Tennyson von zwei grossen
Dichtern stark beeinflusst worden ist, von Shakspere
und, wenn auch in weniger hohem Grade, von Spenser.

Liest man ferner Malory aufmerksam nach und ver-
gleicht sein Werk mit den Idylls, so sieht man, dass diese
der Quelle in sprachlicher Beziehung vieles verdanken.
Unzählige Wörter und Ausdrücke, die Tennyson gebraucht,
sind ohne Zweifel aus dem Einfluss Malorys zu erklären.

Aus der Thatsache, dass Tennyson der Sohn eines
englischen Geistlichen war, dass er in einer Landpfarre
aufwuchs und dort zum Teil seine Bildung empfing, sowie
andrerseits aus dem starken religiösen Zug, der seinem
Wesen eigen war, erklären sich die vielen biblischen Ausdrücke und Gedanken, die in den Idylls vorkommen. Hand
in Hand mit dem zunehmenden Alter des Dichters ging eine
immer stärker hervortretende dramatische Färbung, die er
seinen Dichtungen gab. Die Mehrzahl der Idylls schrieb
er, als er bereits fünfzig Jahre alt war, und als elf der-

selben fertig waren, wandte er sich fast ganz der dramatischen Schriftstellerei zu.

Ich gebe im Folgenden eine Übersicht der mir bekannt gewordenen Litteratur über die Idylls.

"Essay of Tennyson's Idylls of the King", Wissenschaftliche Beilage zum Programm der Luisen-Schule, von Dr. Albert Hamann, Berlin 1887. Gleich am Anfang seines Essay behauptet Dr. Hamann, dass, was Tennyson von Arthur erzählt, aus Malory und den Mabinogion entlehnt ist, aber er macht keinen Versuch, diese Behauptung zu beweisen. Der Essay ist weiter nichts als eine Inhaltsangabe der Idylls.

Dann hat Dr. Wüllenweber (Marburg 1889) eine Dissertation über "Tennysons Königsidylle The Coming of Arthur und ihre Quellen" geschrieben, aber dieselbe handelt nicht von der Sprache des Idylls als solcher. Der Verfasser weist nach, dass Malory die Hauptquelle des Idylls ist, und dass Tennyson ausserdem Ellis, Monmouth und Nennius benutzte. Im zweiten Teile der Abhandlung wird die Art erörtert, wie Tennyson seine Quellen benutzt hat. Dr. Wüllenwebers Arbeit kam mir erst zu Gesicht, als ich mit meiner eigenen vergleichenden Zusammenstellung bereits fertig war. So musste ich schliesslich viele Auszüge, die ich gemacht hatte, bei Seite lassen, da sie bereits von Dr. W. erwähnt waren. Nur die von ihm nicht erwähnten werden in meiner Arbeit aufgeführt.

Im Jahre 1894 hat W. Macculum, Professor der modernen Litteratur an der Universität zu Sydney, ein grosses Werk, über "Tennysons Idylls of the King and Arthurian Story from the 16th Century", veröffentlicht. Dasselbe enthält eine Geschichte der Arthursage von den Celtischen Zeiten an, und eine Darstellung der Art und Weise, wie diese Sage von Nennius, Geoffrey, Wace und Malory behandelt worden ist. Dann folgen verschiedene Capitel über die Zeitgenossen von Tennyson in England und im Auslande und über Tennyson als arthurischen Dichter. Eine allgemeine Interpretation der Idylls und der Anschauungen, die darin enthalten sind, bilden den Schluss des Buches. Die Sprache wird nicht berührt.

Endlich hat Prof. Richard Jones eine Doktor-Dissertation (Heidelberg, Lippincott, Philadelphia 1895) über "The Growth of the Idylls of the King" geschrieben. Zuerst giebt Prof. Jones einen Vergleich zwischen den Idylls und Faust, und, nachdem er von der Entwicklung und Verbreitung der Arthursage gehandelt hat, erörtert er die von Tennyson für die Idylls benutzten Quellen und untersucht eingehend die Frage, ob das Idyll "Merlin and Vivien" irgendwie von Malory abhängig ist. Er kommt zu dem Schluss, dass dies nicht der Fall ist, und spricht die Vermutung aus, dass Tennyson den Stoff zu Vivien "aus dem Mabinogion" von Lady Guest entnahm. Die nächsten Capitel handeln von den Veränderungen, die die späteren Ausgaben der Idylls gegenüber den früheren aufweisen, Veränderungen, die den Zweck haben, den Styl anmutiger zu gestalten und der Erzählung mehr Fülle zu geben. Schliesslich erörtert Prof. Jones kurz den Inhalt der Idylls und die in ihnen vertretenen religiösen Anschauungen.

Vieles andere ist besonders in Zeitschriften, über die Idyllen geschrieben worden, aber alle Verfasser suchen nur die Anschauungen und die Religion des Dichters darzustellen. In den folgenden Artikeln und Essays werden die "Idylls" ihrem Inhalte nach noch behandelt: "Quarterly Review" (Gladstone) London 1859; Edinburgh Review 1870; Macmillan's Magazine (Hutton) London 1872; Elsdale, Studies in the Idylls, London 1878; Nineteenth Century (Traill) London 1892; Nineteenth Century (Knowles) 1893.

Tennyson und die Bibel.

In einigen Fällen finden wir ein einfaches Citat wie auf T. s. 322. "I know thee who thou art", Mark. 1, 24; T. s. 338 "blessed be thou", I Sam. 26. 25; T. s. 366 "the king of Kings", Ezek. 26, 7; T. s. 368 "cast his eyes", Gen. 39, 7 etc. etc. — In anderen Fällen weicht der Ausdruck hinsichtlich der sprachlichen Form so wenig von dem der Bibel ab, dass letztere unzweifelhaft als die Quelle anzusehen ist, z. B. T. s. 361, "I cannot steal . . . no nor beg", vergl. Luke 16, 3, "I cannot dig and to beg I am ashamed"; T. s. 362, "He sickens nigh to death", vergl. Phil. 2, 27, "sick nigh unto death"; T. s. 374, "L. lifted his eyes", vergl. Luke 6, 20. "Jesus lifted up his eyes"; T. s. 377 "arise and hence", vergl. John 14, 31 "Arise, let us go hence"; T. s. 416, "with a love beyond all love in women", vergl. II. Sam. 1, 26, "thy love passing the love of woman". Viele andere Fälle giebt es, in denen die Form einer Redensart aus der Bibel entlehnt wurde, z. B. T. s. 344 "a noise as of a broad brook", vergl. Acts 2, 2, "a sound as of a rushing wind"; T. s. 355. "Here comes a laggard . . . come we will slay him . . . and his damsel shall be ours", vergl. Mark. 12, 7 "This is the heir, come let us kill him, and the inheritance shall be ours"; T. s. 369, "he crowned a happy life with a fair death", vergl. Ps. 65, 11 "crownest a year with goodness". Ausserdem finden sich Anspielungen auf die

biblische Geschichte, bei denen weniger Sprachliches entlehnt ist z. B. T. s. 352 "Neither court nor country, tho
they sought Thro' all the provinces like those of old That
lighted on Queen Esther, has her match", (vergl. Esther
2, 7, "And he brought up Esther, and the maid was fair
and beautiful". Endlich werden viele Worte in rein bib-
lischem Sinne gebraucht, z. B. "prevailed" für „conquered" T. s. 310 „and the kings prevailed"; vergl. Exod.
17, 11 "Israel prevailed"; das Verbum "lift" mit "voice"
oder "eyes", was sich oft findet, s. 311 „lift his voice",
s. 374 "lifted his eyes", auch s. 382 "lifted up his face";
s. 397 das Wort "tale" für "number"; s. 421 "der Ausdruck" it came to pass" für "happened". — Auch findet sich
eine beträchtliche Zahl von Fällen, in denen die Figura
etymologica vorliegt, z. B T. s 380 "sleep the sleep", Jer.
51, 39; T. s. 388 "work thy work", Hab. 1, 5 etc.; T. s.
410 "die the death", Num. 16, 29 etc.; T. s. 428 "vow a
vow", Num. 6, 2 etc.; T. s. 457, "dream a dream", Gen.
37, 5; T. s. 468 "fought a fight", I. Tim. 4, 7 etc., T. s.
473 „live a live", Gal. 2, 20 etc.

Die Wendungen, welche biblisches Gepräge tragen,
habe ich in folgender Liste zusammengefasst.

Coming of Arthur. s. 309. "wasted all the land",
vergl. Jer. 2, 15 "made his land waste, Micah 5, 6; "Arthur
for a space", "space" im Sinne von Zeit, vergl. Acts. 19,
8, "a space of three months", Acts. 19, 10, Lev. 25, 8 etc.;
"between the man and beast", vergl. Gen. 6, 7, "both man
and beast" etc. (der Ausdruck kommt häufig vor). s. 310.
"Saving I be joined with her", "with" für "to", vergl.
Isai. 14, 1, "Strangers be joined with them", Ps 83, 8 etc.;
„the kings prevailed", "prevailed" für „conquered", vergl.
Exod. "Israel prevailed", I. Chron. 5, 2 etc.; "lightnings
and thunders", in der Mehrzahl, Exod. 19, 16, Rev. 16, 18
etc. s. 311. "lifted his voice", vergl. "lift up voice", Job.
38, 34 etc. etc. s. 312. "B. cleaved to Arther", vergl.
Josh. 23, 8, "cleave to the Lord your God", Gen. 2, 24 etc.;

„until his hour should come . . . for his hour had come", vergl. John 2, 4, "mine hour is not yet come", etc.; "wild beasts would have torn the child", vergl. Gen. 31, 39, "Which was torn of beasts", Lev. 22, 8; "Merlin brought Arthur forth and set him in the hall", vergl. Gen. 19, 16, "Angels brought Lot forth and set him etc.", "a hundred voices cried", "Away with him", vergl. John 19, 15, "and they cried out Away with him"; "the king made feast", vergl. Gen. 19, 3, "Lot made feast", Esth. 1, 3 etc.; "as they sat at meat", vergl. Matt. 9, 10, "As Jesus sat at meat", Mark. 2, 15 etc. S. 313. "strait vows", "strait" für "strict", "narrow" Luke 13, 24 etc.; ["comfortable words" vergl. "hear what comfortable words". — Communion Service of English Prayer Book]; "a voice as of the waters" (auch s. 316) vergl Rev. 14, 2, "as the voice of many waters"; "hath power to walk the waters like our Lord"; vergl. Matt. 14, 25, "Jesus went unto them, walking on the sea"; "elfin Urim", Exod. 28, 30, Lev. 8, 84 etc.; the time to cast away is far-off", Eccl. 3, 6, "A time to keep, and a time to cast away". S. 315. "could I part in peace", vergl. Luke 2, 39, "Let thy servant depart in peace"; "dark sayings from of old", vergl. Ps. 78, 2. "utter dark sayings of old". S. 316. "earth b e c a m e a s nothing", vergl. Gen. 3, 22. "Man is b e c o m e a s one of us"; "latter April", ähnlicher Gebrauch von "latter", Job. 19, 25, "latter day", Prov. 16, 15 etc.

Gareth and Lynnette. S. 318. "Yea, well-beloved", vergl. Mark. 12, 6, "He sent his well-beloved son" etc.; "B. bemoaned himself", bemoan als Reflexiv., vergl. Jer. 31, 18, E. bemoan himself. S. 319. "an o f t e n c h a n c e"; o f t e n als Adjektiv, vergl. I. Tim. 5, 23, "thine often in-firmities"; "I was f r e q u e n t with him", für "frequently", vergl. II. Corr. "I am in prisons more frequent". S. 330. "to serve for m e a t s and d r i n k s", vergl. Heb. 9, 10, "Stood only in meats and drinks"; Ps. 71, 20, Rom. 8, 11 etc. S. 321. "We have heard from our wise men", vergl. Eccl. 9, 7 "words of wise men are heard"; "No gate under heaven", vergl. Gen. 1, 19, "waters under heaven", Acts. 2, 5 etc. etc.; "tillers of the soil", vergl. Gen. 4, 2 "Cain was a tiller of ground"; "here is truth", truth ohne Artikel häufig Deut. 13, 14. "If it be truth" etc.; "that Seer made answer", Deut. 20, 11, "make answer". S. 322. "Some there be that hold", vergl. Matt. 7, 14, "Few there be that find"; "but I know thee who thou art", Mark. 1, 24 "I know thee who thou art", auch Luke 4, 34. S. 323. "the tree was pleasant in my husband's eyes", vergl. Gen. 3, 6. "the tree was pleasant to the eyes"; "get thee hence", I. Kings 17, 3 "Get thee hence", auch Matt. 4, 10. S. 324. "rend the cloth", vergl. Lev. 10, 6 "rend your clothes", auch II. Chron. 34, 27; "We stayed their hands", II. Sam. 24, 16, "Stay thine hand", I. Chron. 21, 15. S. 325. "draw water, or hew wood", vergl. Josh. 9, 21 "let them be hewers of wood, and drawers of water". S. 326. "uttermost obedience", uttermost häufig II. King 7, 5, Neh. 1, 9 etc. "God willing", Rom. 9, 22; "wherefore would ye men should wonder", Mark. 10, 36, vergl. "What would ye I should do". S. 327. "a lady of great lands", "lands im Sinne von Güter", Neh. 5, 3; "mindful of Sir Gareth", vergl. Ps. 115, 12, "mindful of us", Ps. 8, 4; "never a whit", 2. Cor. 11, 5, "not a whit". S. 329. "the villain lifted up his voice", Job. 38, 34 "lift up voice to clouds", Isa. 24, 14 etc.; "by God's grace", II. Cor. 1, 12, "by grace of God", I. Cor. 15, 10 etc. S. 330. "G. loosed the stone from off his neck", Josh. 5, 15, "Loose thy shoe from off thy feet"; "six men haling a seventh", "hale" für "haul", Acts. 8, 3, "Saul hale men to prison"; "Whatsoever ye say", Num. 22, 17, "Whatsoever thou sayest"; "in the deeps", "deep" als Substantiv, Ps. 88, 6" in the deeps", Neh. 9, 11 etc.; "to bide with thee", "bide" für "abide", Rom. 11, 23; "G. loosed his bonds", Job. 12, 18, "he looseth the bond". S. 331. "with a stone about his neck", Matt. 18, 6, "It were better that a millstone were hanged abont his neck". S. 332. "have I done the deed", I. Cor. 5, 2, "hath done this deed" etc.; "look thou to thyself", im Sinne von "take care of", II John 8, "look to yourselves". S. 333. "well-stricken", Gen. 18, 11 und 24, 1. S. 334. "hear a parable of the knave", Matt. 13, 18, "Hear ye a parable of the sower". S. 335. "Where-withal", Matt. 6, 31. S. 336. "Well done, knave-knight", Matt. 25, 21, "well done, faithful servant."; "thou hast made us lords", Gen. 27, 37, "I have made him thy lord"; "brake it utterly", Jsai. 24, 10, "utterly broken". S. 337. "baken meats", Gen. 40. 17, "bake-meats", I. Kings 19, 6 "baken". S. 338. "L. said", Blessed be thou" I. Sam. 26, 25, "Saul said" "Blessed be thou"; "And when reviled hast answered graciously", vergl. I. Cor. 4, 12, "being reviled, we bless"; "seek, till we find", vergl. Matt. 7, 7, "Seek and ye shall find". S. 339. "Peradventure he may know", "peradventure" ein echt bibl. Wort, Gen. 18, 24 "perad-venture there be", I. Kings 18, 4 etc.; "hath wrought on L. vergl. Matt. 26, 10, "She hath wrought on me"; "his anger tare him", Mark. 9, 20 "the spirit tare him". S. 340. "throughly" für "thoroughly", Job. 6, 2 etc.

Marriage of Geraint. S. 342. "He compassed her with sweet observances", Ps. 32, 7 "compass me with songs"; „she thought to tell", "to" für "of", Gen. 48, 11. "I had not thought to see", Num. 33, 56; "I gird his harness on him", "harness" für "armour" I. Kings. 20, 11 "him girdeth on his harnass". S. 344. "Thon art not worthy to speak to him", vergl. Mark. 1, 7 "I am not worthy to unloose" und Rev. 5, 9. "Thou art worthy to take"; "a noise as of a broad brook" vergl. Acts. 2, 2. "A sound as of a rushing wind". S. 345. "ancient churl", "ancient" im Sinne von "old", für Personen die noch leben. Ezra 2, 3, "ancient men Ezek. 9, 6 etc. S. 346. "Make us merry", Rev. 11, 10 und Judg. 9, 27 etc.; "Buy us flesh and wine, and we will make us merry", vergl. Luke 15, 27 "Bring hether the fatted calf, and kill it, and let us eat

and make merry"; "buy us flesh and wine", vergl. II. Sam.
6, 19, "a good piece of flesh and a flagon of wine", Dan.
10, 3, "neither flesh nor wine in mouth". S. 347. „the
wine made summer", Ps. 74, 17 "thou hast made summer",
„art thou he", Jer. 14, 22 "Art thou not he". S. 348.
"gold which was not rendered to him", "render" im Sinne
wie "give". II. Chron. 6, 30. "render to every man" Ps.
28, 4 etc. S. 352. "that appertains to maintenance", "appertains" wo jetzt "pertains" gebraucht wird, Num. 16, 32
"that appertains to Korak"; "neither court nor country,
tho' they sought Thro' all the provinces like those of old
That lighted on Queen Esther, has her match". Esther
2, 7. "And he brought up Esther, and the maid was fair
and beautiful".

Geraint and Enid. S. 354. "Where we see as we
are seen", vergl. I. Cor. 13, 12. "Then shall I know as
I am known. S. 355. "Here comes a laggard . . . come
we will slay him . . . and his damsel shall be ours", vergl.
Mark. 12, 7 "This is the heir, come. let us kill him, and
the inheritance shall be ours"; "they would slay you, and
possess your horse", "possess" im Sinne wie "take possession
of", vergl. Deut. 1, 21, "Go up and possess the land".
S. 356. "Cleave to the better man", Gen. 2, 24, "cleave to
his wife", Deut. 4, 4; "to confound them more", "confound"
im Sinne wie "put to confusion" Jsac. 37, 27 "inhabitants
were confounded. S. 357. "died the death" Matt. 15, 4;
"victual", die Einzahl wird nicht mehr gebraucht, Ex. 12,
39, "prepared victual" etc.; fare meet for mowers", Hebr.
6, 7 "herbs meet for them". S. 359. "of waste and
wilderness", Deut. 32, 10 "in a waste wilderness", Job. 30,
3 etc.; "Right well I know", Ps 139, 14 "My soul knoweth
right well". S. 360. "thy reckoning", "reckoning" im
Sinne von "bill", II. Kings 22, 7 "no reckoning made".
S. 361. "and ears to hear", Ezek. 12, 2, "they have ears
to hear", Matt. 11, 15 etc.; "I cannot steal . . . no nor
beg", vergl. Luke 16, 3 "I cannot dig, and to beg I am

ashamed". S. 362. "He sickens, nigh to death", vergl. Phil. 2, 27 "sick nigh unto death"; "At the point of noon", Gen. 25, 32, "I am at the point to die", John 4, 47, "At the point of death"; Your wailing will not quicken him", "quicken" im Sinne von "bring to life", Rom. 4, 17 "God who quickeneth dead"; "comely face", vergl. Cant. 2, 14, "thy countenance is comely". S. 363. "on an oaken settle", "settle" als "seat" Ezek. 43, 14 "lower settle" etc.; "feigned himself", reflex. I. Sam. 21, 13. "D. feigned himself"; "called for flesh and wine", vergl. Dan. 10, 3. "neither flesh nor wine". S. 364. "Who took no thought of them", Matt. 6, 25, "take no thought for your life", Mark. 13, 11 etc. S. 366. "The king of Kings", Ezek. 26, 7, auch I. Tim. 6, 15. S. 368. "and cast his eyes" Gen. 39, 7 "master's wife cast eyes on J."; "he looked and found them wanting", vergl. Dan. 5, 27 "Thou art weighed in the balance and found wanting". S. 369. "he rested well content", vergl. Prov. 6, 35, "nor will he rest content.", "till he crowned a happy life with a fair death", vergl. Ps. 65, 11, "crownest a year with goodness.

Balin and Balan. S. 369. "why sat ye", vergl. Acts. 1, 11. "Why stand ye". S. 370. "spoken evil of me", John 18, 23, "spoken evil", Mark. 9, 39 etc.; "those years were wormwood-bitter", vergl. Prov. 5, 4, "her end was bitter as wormwood"; "the Lost one found was greeted as in Heaven with joy", vergl. Luke 15. 6 "Rejoice for I have found that which was lost"; "in the name of Christ", Acts. 3, 6. "in the name of Jesus Christ"; "the Saint Arimathean Joseph", vergl. John 19. 38 "Joseph of Arimathea, a disciple of Christ. S. 371. "that same spear wherewith the Roman pierced the side of Christ", vergl. John 19, 34 "And one of the soldiers with a spear pierced his side". S. 372. "golden earnest of a gentler life", "Earnest" als Hauptwort II. Cor. 1, 22, "the earnest of the Spirit". S. 374. "L. lifted his eyes", vergl. Luke 6, 20. "J. lifted

his eyes". S. 375. "he caught his hand away" vgl. Acts.
8, 39, "the Spirit caught away Philip". S. 376. "a cry
sounded", vergl. Jer. 51, 54. "A sound of a cry cometh";
"stay him", "stay" als transitives Zeitwort, II. Sam. 24,
16, I. Chron. 21, 15 etc. S. 377. "lord of all things"
vergl. Gen. 42, 10, "lord of the land", Gen. 45, 8, "lord
of all his house"; "arise and hence" John 14, 31, "Arise
let us go hence". S. 378. "evil spirit upon him leapt",
I. Sam. 16, 16 "evil spirit is upon thee". S. 379. "What
manner of men they be". I. Thes 1, 4, "Ye know what,
manner of men"; "I better prize the living dog than the
dead lion", vergl. Eccles. 9, 4, "a living dog is better than
a dead lion". S. 380. "the night has come", John 9, 4
"night cometh"; and slept the sleep", Ps. 13, 3 "Lest I
sleep the sleep".

Merlin and Vivien. S. 380. "but neither marry nor
are given in marriage, angels of our Lord's report", Matt.
22, 30. "They neither marry nor are given in marriage,
and are as the angels of God in Heaven". S. 381. "As
love, if love be perfect, casts out fear", I. John 4, 18,
"There is no fear in love, but perfect love casteth out
fear"; "there is no being pure", vergl. Prov. 20, 9, "Who
can say, I am pure from sin"; "and the damsel bidden
rise arose", vergl. Mark. 5, 42 "and the damsel arose".
S. 382. "forgotten of the Queen", "of" statt "by", Job.
28, 4 "waters forgotten of the foot"; "as A. in the
highest", Luke 2, 16. "Glory to God in the highest";
"they lifted up their faces", II. Kings 9, 32, "lift up face"
Ezra 9, 2 etc. S. 388. "work my work", Hab. 1, 5. "I
will work a work. S. 391. "wreathen" II. Kings 25, 17
"wreathen work". S. 392. "the spotless Lamb of Christ",
I. Peter 1, 19, "a lamb without spot"; "flustered with new
wine", vergl. Acts. 2, 13. "these men are full of new wine".
S. 394. "seethed like a kid in its own mother's milk", vergl.
Ex. 23, 19. "thou shall not seethe a kid in his mother's
milk"; "henceforward evermore", Jsa. 59, 21, "henceforth

and for ever". S. 395. "she called him lord", I. Pet. 3, 6, "calling him lord".

Lancelot and Elaine. S. 396. "and rolled his enemy down". Jer. 51, 25" I will roll thee down"; "thou shalt be king", I. Kings. 11, 37, "thou shalt be king over Israel". S. 397. "tale of diamonds", "tale" im Sinne von "Anzahl", Ex. 5. 8. "tale of bricks". S. 399. "nay, good father". Luke 16, 30 "nay, father Abraham"; "who was a living soul", I. Cor. 15, 45, "A. was made a living soul"; "His mood was like a fiend and drave him into wastes and solitudes" vgl. Luke 8, 29. "And he brake his bonds, and was driven of the devil into the wilderness". S. 400. "loved of the loveliest", "of" statt "by" nach dem Verbum, häufig in der Bibel, vgl. Luke 8, 29 "driven of the devil", Isa. 53, 4, "smitten of God", Rom. 13, 1 "ordained of God" [auf S. 405 kommt "wearied of the quest" vor]; "on the mount of Badon, Zech. 14, 4 "on the mount of Olives"; "the fire of God fills him", Job. 1, 16, "the fire of God is fallen". S. 404 "stanched", "a" für "au", Luke 8, 44 "stanched". S. 407. "Must our true man change like a leaf". Isa. 64, 6. "We all do change as a leaf"; "all tongues loosed", vgl. Mark. 7, 35, "his tongue was loosed"; "fire in dry stubble", Job. 13, 25 "Pursue dry stubble". S. 410. "had died the death", Num. 23, 10, "let me die the death"; "born of sickness", vgl. John. 3, 4 "born of water, born of flesh, John. 1, 13 etc. S. 411. "I will endow you even to the half of my realm", vgl. Mark. 6, 23. "Whatsoever thou shalt ask I will give it thee, even to the half of my kingdom". S. 412. "Have comfort", auch Job. 6, 10; "Peace be to thee", Judg. 6, 23 etc. S. 413 "mock at me", Lam. 1, 7, "mock at her"; "in an open shame", Heb. 6, 6. "To an open shame". S. 414. "servitor", II. King. 4, 43; "have my joy", kommt mehrere Mal vor, Ps. 17, 21, Isa. 9, 17 etc S. 415. "done despite", Hebr. 10, 29; "the mother of our Lord", Luke 1, 43. S. 416 "But loved me with a love beyond all love in women", vgl. II. Sam. 1, 26 "Thy love to me was wonderful passing, the love of women". S. 418. "What profits me my name", vgl. Mark. 8, 36. "What shall it profit a man"; "break these bonds", Jer. 5, 5. "burst the bonds". S. 419. "The cup itself, from which our Lord drank at the last Supper with his own" vgl. Matt. 26, 27, "And he took the cup and gave thanks saying", "Drink ye all of it"; "after the day of darkness, when the dead went wandering o'er Moriah", vgl. Matt. 27, 53. "And many bodies came out of the graves after the resurrection and went into the city"; "and if a man could touch it or see it, he was healed at once, by faith, of all his ills", vgl. Mark. 5, 28, "if I may but touch his clothes. I shall be whole", und Matt. 9, 22, "thy faith hath made thee whole"; "was caught away to Heaven", vgl. II. Cor. 12, 4 "He was caught up into Paradise" und Acts 8, 39, "The Spirit caught away Philip". S. 420. "adulterous race", Matt. 12, 39. "an adulterous generation"; "to me by prayer and fasting", Matt. 17, 21. "by prayer and fasting"; "I heard a sound as of a silver horn", Acts. 2, 2, "I heard a sound as of a rushing wind"; "and myself fasted and prayed", Acts. 13, 3 "they had fasted and prayed"; "the holy thing is here", vgl. Luke 1, 35, "that holy thing born of thee. S. 421 "sister or brother none had he", vgl. Acts. 3, 6, "Silver and gold have I none"; "it came to pass", häufig in der Bibel für "it happened", Exod. 12, 41 etc.; "if I lose myself I save myself", vgl. Matt. 10, 39, "He that loseth his life for my sake shall find it". S. 423 "woe is me", Ps. 120, 5 etc.; "What go ye into the wilderness to see", vgl. Matt. 11, 7 "What went ye out into the wilderness to see?"; "And all the blind shall see", vgl. Isa. 29, 18, "And the eyes of the blind shall see". S. 424 "And I was lifted up in heart", Lam. 3, 41, "Let us lift up our hearts". S. 425 "the Lord of all the world", vgl. Jer. 32, 37 "I am the Lord of all flesh"; "exceeding age" "exceeding" als Adjectiv öfters Ps. 43, 4 "exceeding joy" etc. S. 426 "Thou hast not true humility, For when the Lord of all things made himself Naked of glory for his mortal change", vgl. Phil. 2, 7—8, "And Christ Jesus took upon himself the form of a servant, and was made in the likeness of men, and being found in fashion as a man, he humbled himself"; "And like a flying star led on the gray-haired wisdom of the East"; vgl. Matt. 2, 2, "We have seen his star in the East"; "When the hermit made an end" (of speaking), öfters in der Bibel, Deut. 32, 45, etc. "made an end of speaking"; "I saw the Holy Grail descend upon the shrine", Matt. 3, 22. "And the Holy Ghost descended upon him"; "face as of a child", Rev. 4, 7, "face as of a man"; "My time is hard at hand", Matt. 26, 18, "My time is at hand". S. 427 "All the Heavens opened", Mark. 1, 10, "He saw the Heavens opened"; "Shoutings of all the sons of God"; Job. 38, 7 "All the sons of God shouted for joy"; "The veil had been withdrawn", II. Cor. 3, 16, "The veil had been taken away"; "I saw the spiritual city and all her spires And gateways in a glory like one pearl", Rev. 21, 10 und 21 "and shewed me that great city . . . . and the twelve gates were 12 pearls, every several gate was of one pearl". S. 428 "or vowed a vow", Gen. 28, 20 "Jacob vowed a vow"; "Arthur's warning word", Exod. 12, 35 "word of Moses", "word" für "words"; "there is a lion in the way", Prov. 22, 13 "there is a lion in the way". S. 429 "a maid loosed and let him go", John 11, 44, "loose him and let him go". S. 430 "as they trode", trode für trod immer in der Bibel, Judg. 20, 43, trode grapes etc.; "a gale made havoc", Acts 8, 3, "Saul made havock"; "I communed with a man", I. Sam. 18, 22, "communed with David" etc.; "Perhaps like him of Cana in Holy Writ, Our Arthur kept his best until the last", John 2, 10. "Every man at the beginning doth set forth good wine, and when men have well drunk, then that which is worse, but thou hast kept the good wine until now"; "perils in the storm", 2. Cor. 11, 26, "perils of waters". S. 431. "to be plucked asunder",

Mark. 5, 4. "Chains plucked asunder"; "in the great sea wash away thy sin", Acts. 22, 16. "and wash away thy sins". S. 432. "Glory and joy and honour to our Lord", 1. Tim. 1, 17. "to God be honour and glory"; "there came a sign from heaven", Mark. 8. 11. "Seeking a sign from heaven"; "Whereto see thou", Matt. 27, 4. "See thou to that". S. 433. "Nor that One who rose again", Luke 24, 6 "He is not here but is risen"; "Ye have seen what ye have seen", ähnliche Construction, John 19, 22, "What I have written I have written".

Peleas and Ettarre. S. 433. "lately come to his inheritance", Ps. 79, 1, "heathen are come into thine inheritance"; "for fair thou art", Cant. 1, 15, "thou art fair", Cant. 7, 5, "how fair thou art". S. 435. "wonder after" für "wonder at", Rev. 13, 3. S. 436. "small matter", Gen. 30, 15, "Is it a small matter"; "all manner of", "all manner" für "every manner" öfters Exod. 1, 14 etc. S. 437. "thou fool", Matt. 5, 22; 1. Cor, 15, 36. S. 440. "Would they have risen against me", Jer. 51, 1, "them that rise up against me"; "Before high God", Ps. 78, 35, Dan. 4, 2 etc. S. 441. "That own no lust, because they have no law", Rom. 7, 7. "For I had not known lust, except the law had said"; "with living waters", Jer. 2, 13, "Forsaken living waters", auch Jer. 17, 13. S. 443. "loose thy tongue", Mark. 7, 35. "the string of his tongue was loosed"; "the time is hard at hand, "Rev. 1, 3, "for the time is at hand".

The Las Tournament. S. 444 "my Churl for whom Christ died", Rom. 14, 15, "Destroy not him for whom Christ died"; "Man was it, who marred heaven's image", Gen. 1, 27, "God created man in his own image". S. 445. "Lancelot is it well", 2. King. 4, 26, "Is it well with thee"; "They stood without the doors", Gen. 24, 31, "wherefore standest thou without"; "a sound is in his ears", Job. 15, 21, "a dreadful sound is in his ears"; "lifted up her head", Gen. 40, 13, "Shall lift up thine

head", auch Job. 10, 15 etc. S. 446 "Fair damsels"
1 King 1, 4, "A. was a fair damsel". S. 448 "Fear God,
honour the king", 1, Pet. 2, 17 "Fear God, honour the
king"; "blasted grain", 2. Kings 19, 26 "as corn blasted"
auch Isa. 37, 27; "I have flung thee pearls, and find thee
swine", Matt. 7, 6, "Neither cast ye pearls before swine".
S. 449 "He can make figs out of thistles", Matt. 7, 16,
"Do men gather figs of thistles". S. 451 "they hurled the
tables over", Matt. 21, 12, "Jesus overthrew the tables";
"As the water Moab saw", 2. Kings. 3, 22, "the Moabites
saw the water"; "Till one lone woman, weeping near a
cross, stayed him", "Why weep ye"? "Lord", "she said, my
man hath left me or is dead", vgl. Job 20, 11 und 13,
"But Mary stood without at the sepulchre . . . and they
say unto her", "Woman why weepest thou", "She saith
unto them", "because they have taken away my lord".
S. 452 "the measure of my hate", Matt. 23, 32, "the measure
of your favour".

Guinevere. S. 457 "She dreamed an awful dream",
Gen. 37, 5, "J. dreamed a dream"; "Get thee hence" [auch
S. 461], 1. Kings. 17, 3, "Get thee hence"; "lionlike leapt",
2. Sam. 23, 20, "lionlike men". S. 458 "He set her
thereon" ("on the horse"), Matt. 21, 7, "they set him
thereon" ("on the ass"). S. 459 "I cry my cry", Gen. 27,
34 "Esau cried with a bitter cry"; "her foolish prate",
Prov. 10, 8, "a prating fool"; "signs and wonders", Acts.
7, 36, "shewed signs and wonders", auch Acts. 14, 3 etc.
S. 460 "they stayed him up", Ex. 17, 12, "A. and H.
stayed up his hands". S. 462 "goodliest man", 1. Sam. 8,
16, "goodliest young men". S. 463 "kith and kin clave to
him", Neh. 10, 29, "they clave to their brethren"; "bear
with me", "bear with" im Sinne von "Mitleid haben",
2. Cor. 11, 4, "ye might bear with him"; "swear to reverence
the King", 1. King. 1, 31. „B. reverenced the King"; "uphold
the Christ", Ps. 119, 116, "Uphold me (Lord) according
to word". S. 463 "ensample" für "example", Phil.

— 26 —

3. 17, 2. Thes. 3, 9 etc. S. 464 "I did not come to curse
thee", Num. 23, 13 "come . . . and curse me then"; "And
in the flesh thon hast sinned", Rom. 7, 25 "with flesh I
serve law of sin", Rom. 8, 3, "sinful flesh"; "We may
meet before high God", Amos 4, 12. "Prepare to meet.
thy God"; "I hear the trumpet blow", Isa. 18, 3. "When
he bloweth trumpet hear ye". S. 465 "So she did not see
the face which then was as an angel's", Acts. 6, 15, "All
saw his face as it had been the face of an angel"; "My
lord, the king" kommt 1. Sam. 26, 17, Jer. 38, 9 etc. vor;
"high God" in Ps. 78, 35, Dan. 4, 2. S. 466 "wrought the
ruin", Prov. 26, 28, "worketh ruin".

The Passing of Arthur. S. 467 "And in His ways
with men"; Job. 34, 21. "His eyes are upon the ways of
men"; "My God thou hast forgotten me", Ps. 22, 1. "My
God why hast thou forgotten me", auch Mark. 15, 34.
S. 468 "After the Christ", Christ mit bestimmtem Artikel,
Matt. 16, 20; 26, 63 etc. etc S. 468 "In the battle, oaths
. . . and monstrous blasphemies", in der Schlacht von
Armageddon, Rev. 16, 19, "they blasphemed the name of
God"; "fought a fight", 2. Tim. 4, 7, "fought a good fight".
S. 469 "That quick or dead", "quick" im Sinne von "living",
2. Tim. 4, 1, "quick and dead", auch 1. Pet. 4, 5 etc.;
"days of old", Ps. 77, 5 ; Ps. 143, 5. S. 470 "many-knotted
waterflags"; in der Bibel wird "flag" für "waterflag" gebraucht, Isa. 19, 6 "reeds and flags", Ex. 2, 3 etc.; "lightly
bring me word", lightly" im Sinne von "quickly", Jer. 4,
24, "hills moved lightly"; "it is not meet to leave thee",
"meet" für "right", Matt. 15, 26 "it is not meet to take".
S. 471 "curiously chased", Ps. 139, 15 "curiously wrought".
S. 472 "they were ware", ware für aware Acts. 14, 6.
S. 473 "I have lived my life", Gal. 2, 20, "the life which
I now live". S. 474 "I will heal me of my wound", Jer.
30, 17, "I will heal thee of thy wounds".

Vergleich mit Shakespere

Wir sahen bisher, dass die "Idylls of the King" mit biblischen Ausdrücken und Citaten stark durchsetzt sind. Wir können weiter beobachten, dass sie sprachlich entschieden einen dramatischen, speziell Shakespere'schen Zug haben. In Betracht kommt hier:

1. Der häufige und regelmässige Gebrauch solcher Wörter wie s o für i f, e n o w für e n o u g h, a n für if, b e l i k e, a v a u n t, b e g o n e, a y, a y für y e s, a y zur Verstärkung der Bedeutung, m e t h i n k s, i t b e s e e m e t h, g o o d n o w (als ganzer Satz), G o d's m e r c y, und p r a y h e a v e n als Ausrufe, a n o n, w h e r e w i t h a l, O f i e, m a r k für p e r c e i v e, n o t i c e, c h e e r als Hauptwort, l o o n!, t h y p a r d o n (absolut), weal etc.

2. Der häufige Gebrauch des Singulars statt des Plurals in Ausdrücken wie: "pleasant in my e y e, for s e r v i c e done, he gave o r d e r, with s t o r e of a p p a r e l, a piece of turret s t a i r, v i c t u a l" etc.

3. Ausdrücke wie: "delivering that" für "saying that", w i t für j u d g m e n t, they had talk, he had longing, they had sport, good cousin and good lord (in der Anrede).

4. Der eigentümliche Gebrauch von Präpositionen, der ebenfalls für Shakspere's Sprache charakteristisch ist, z. B. "to have power o n (für over), to laugh u p o n (für at), to serve f o r (für serve a s), know thee f o r, hail him f o r, die o f (für through), rate a t (für rate), have a t

thee (für take care, guard yourself), but in (für go in), seize on her (für seize), look on (für look at), cry from out (für out of), cry out upon (für exclain against), from out the tower (für out of), cry on help (für cry for).

5. Die häufige Auslassung des Artikels und anderer Wörter z. B. "I must hence" (für go hence), S. 317 "then was latter April" (für then it was), S. 319, "else wherefore born" (für art thou born), "but felt him mine (für to be mine), S. 320, "hence will I" (für will I go), S. 323, "give me to right" (für give me permission to), S. 315, "the King!" (für it is the King) S. 313, "were pale as" (für were as pale as).

6. Die Verwendung der persönlichen Fürwörter "thou, ye, you", wie bei Shakespere, vgl. Abbott, §§ 231—236. Mit "thou" reden sich intime Freude an, der Herr gebraucht "thou" gegenüber dem Diener, z. B. sagt der König zum Kämmerer S. 311, "knowest thou"; ferner thun es die Eltern gegenüber ihren Kindern, z. B. S. 319 redet die Königin B. ihren Sohn Gareth mit "stay thou" an. Auch im Zorne gebraucht man die Anrede "thou", z. B. "What doest thou, scullion"; ebenso gestatten sich Herolde gegenüber Königen das trauliche "thou", z. B. sagt Alfred's Bote, den er zu König L. schickt "If I in aught have served thee"; vgl. bei Shakspere die Anrede des Herolds an Heinrich V. (4, 7, 74), wo ebenfalls "thou" angewandt ist.

Ye involvirt eine gewisse Formalität der Anrede, z. B. S. 330. "damsel whatso'er ye will.

You als Nominativ drückt einen hohen Grad von Achtung aus, z. B. S. 334 "Fair damsel you should worship", S. 339, "wherefore damsel you cannot".

Die Zusammenstellung, die wir folgen lassen, wird die Thatsache deutlich herausstellen, dass eine grosse Zahl von Ausdrücken, die in einer speziellen Bedeutung gebraucht sind, sich ähnlich bei Shakspere findet, und wir sind daher wohl zu dem Schluss berechtigt, dass letzterer auf Tennysons Sprache grossen Einfluss ausgeübt hat (nicht nur was den Satzbau betrifft, sondern auch hinsichtlich des eigentümlichen Gebrauches vieler Worte).

Coming of Arthur.

S. 309. "marked not", mark im Sinne von notice, perceive, be aware of, kommt oft vor Mcb. 1, 2, 28, Caes. 1, 2, 120 etc.

S. 310. "to colleague" = to ally, ein Fall, Hml. 1, 2, 21; "to have power on this land", für power over, Cymb. 5, 5, 418 etc.; "saving" für "except", John I, 201; "trumpet-blast", vgl. trumpet-clangor H 4 B 5, 5, 42.

S. 311. "he laughed upon his warrior", "laugh upon" für "laugh significantly", LLL 5, 2, 472, and Shr. 4, 4, 76; "I know thee for my king", für "I recognize thee as", LLL 5, 2, 131; As. 4, 1, 136 etc. "each warded either", "ward" für "protect" Troil. 1, 2, 292, Tit. 3, 1, 195; "new-made knight", "new-made", John 1, 1, 187, Merch. 2, 6, 6 etc., vgl. new-killed Lucr. 457, new-added Caes. 4, 3, 209; "after-years", vgl. after-hours R 3 IV. 4. 293, after-times H. 4 B. 4, 2, 51.

S. 312· "so ye care"; so häufig gebraucht von Tennyson für if etc., auch bei Shaks. Ado 2, 1, 91, Mids. 3, 2, 314 etc.; "compassed" für encompassed = encircle, surround, Troil. 1, 3, 276 etc.; "enforced" für "forced", Gent. 2, 6, 3 etc.; "not many moons", "moons" für "months", Oth. 1, 3, 84 etc.; "ancient friends", "ancient" im Sinne von "old", bezogen auf eine Person, die noch lebt, "ancient gentleman" Hml. 5, 1, 33 etc.; "they banded" für "banded together", H. 6, A.3, 1, 81.

S. 313. "body", im Sinne von "army, armed force", H. 4, B. 1, 3, 66; "strait vows", "strait" für "strict", Meas, 2, 1, 9 etc.; "enow" für "enough", Merch. 3, 5, 24, H. 5 IV, 1, 24 etc.; "comfortable words", "comfortable" für "comforting", derselbe Ausdruck, R. 2 II, 2, 76. Er kommt im englischen Gebetbuch auch vor. "to cheer his

Table Round", "Table" für "Gesellschaft", Cor. 2, 1, 91, Mcb. 3, 4, 89 etc.; "flame-colour", vgl. "flame-coloured", H. 4, A. 1, 2, 11.

S. 314. "he thought to sift", "thought" im Sinne von "expect, hope", Ado. 2, 3, 236 etc.; "cry from out the dawning", "from out" für "out of", Merch. 3, 4, 21, John 5, 2, 136 etc.; "tell thee true", "true" für "truly", Gent. 2, 5, 35 etc., vgl. "say true" Sonn. 114, 3, "speak true", As. 5, 4, 82 etc.; "a bank of heath", "heath" für "heather", Temp. 1, 1, 70; "a fairy changeling", "changeling, a child left or taken by fairies in place of another", Mids. 2, 1, 23 etc.

S. 315. "sayings from of old", "of old", Tit. 3, 2, 83 etc.; "hail him for their king", "hail for" für "hail as", Meb. 3, 1, 60.

S. 316. "latter April", "latter" für "latter part", vgl. "latter Spring", H. 4, A. 1, 2, 177; "latter day", H. 5 IV, 1, 143; "make the world other", "other" für otherwise", Ado 1, 1, 176, Cor. 4, 6, 102 etc.

S. 317. "for a space", "space" für "time", Per. 4, 1, 68 etc.; "wit" für "judgment, understanding", Gent. 1, 1, 47 etc. etc.

Gareth and Lynette.

S. 317. "prisoned" für "imprisoned", Lucr. 642 etc.; "Heaven yield her for it", "yield" für "reward, bless". Ant. 4, 2, 33, "the gods yield you for it".

S. 318. "discaged", vgl. "discase", Tp. V. 85, disbranch Lo. 4, 2, 34 etc.; "an ye love, an I could", etc., an wird oft für if gebraucht wie by Shaks., vgl. Ado 1, 1, 80, Mids. 1, 2, 58 etc. etc.; "a leash of kings", vgl. "a leash of drawers", H. 6, A. 2, 4, 7; "bemoaned herself", reflex. H. 6, C. 2, 5, 110.

S. 319. "nor sees, nor hears" für "neither . . . nor", viele Fälle, Ven. 1082, Gent. 5, 4, 80 etc.; "an often chance", "often" als Adject. oft in Shaks., As. 4, 1, 19 etc.; "nor fronted man", "front" im Sinne von "face, meet,

oppose", Ant. 1, 4, 79 etc.; "they died of her" für "die
through", Mids. 2, 1, 135, "she of that boy did die"; "comfortable bride", vgl. "comfortable friar", Rom. 5, 3, 148;
"I was frequent with him", "frequent" as "intimate" kommt
einmal vor Sonn. 17, 4; "easeful biding", "easeful" als
"quiet, comfortable", H. 6, C. 5, 3, 6, "biding" im Sinne
von "abode", Lucr. 550 etc.; "kingly speak", "kingly" als
Adverbium, Sonn. 114, 10.

S. 320. "a twelvemonth and a day", auch LLL 5,
2, 837 und 887; "villain kitchen-vassalage", villain als
Adjectiv Merch. 2, 8, 4, Rom. 3, 2, 101 etc.; "princely-proud", princely als Adverb. H. 4, B. 2, 2, 12; "the live
green", "live" für "living", Mids. 2, 1, 172; "spires
pricked thr' the mist", pricked im Sinne von "point,
raise, Tp. IV, 176.

S. 321. "The second echoed him", "echo" to echo
a person, vgl. "he echoes me", Oth. 3, 3, 106; "co-twisted",
vgl. "co-mingle", Hml. 3, 2, 74, co-join Wint. 1, 2, 143,
co-act Troil. 5, 2, 118.

S. 322. "utter truth", "utter" im Sinne von "complete,
pure" H. 6, A. 5, 4, 112 etc.; "fair-spoken" H. 8 IV, 2,
52, "riddling" als Verbum, Mids. 2, 2, 53 etc.; "with good
cheer", cheer für cheerfulness Sonn. 97, 13, Ado 1, 3, 74
etc.; "healthful people", healthful für healthy, Sonn. 118,
11 etc.; "delivering doom", doom für "judgment", Lucr.
717 etc.

S. 323. "he reft a field from", "reft from" im Sinne
von "deprive of", Err. 1, 1, 116 etc.; "howsoe'er at first",
"howsoe'er" für "although", Meas. 2, 1, 231 etc.; "pleasant
in my eye", sing. form für "sight", Compl. 247 etc.
"standeth seized of that inheritance", eigentümlicher
Gebrauch von "seized of" = possessed of, es kommt einmal bei Sh. vor, Hml. 1, 1, 89; "wreak me" für revenge,
Tit. 4, 3, 51 etc.; "thy loves and hates", zwei abstracte
Hauptwörter in der Mehrzahl gebraucht, "loves" Gent. 5,

4, 171 etc., "hates" Troil. 5, 10, 27 etc.; "many of evil savour", "savour" als "repute", Ven. 747 etc.

S. 324. "delivering that" = "saying that", Gent. 1. 1, 138, Err. 2, 2, 166 etc.; "he was ev'n on the way". "ev'n" als "just", Ven. 1025 etc.; "his goodly cousin", "goodly" als "fair, fine", oft sowohl bei T. als bei Sh. Lucr. 1247 etc.; "yield this honour", "yield" als "give, grant". Tp. 1, 2, 309; "to stay their hands from", "to stay from" für "restrain, keep back", Merch. 3, 2, 24 etc.; "lap him in cloth", "lap" als "wrap up, envelope", Macb. 1, 2, 54 etc. (das Wort wird im Norden von England noch gebraucht); "hunger worn", vgl. "hunger-starved", H. 6, C. 1, 4, 5; "more like are we to reave", "like" für "likely", öfters Ado 3, 3, 190 etc.

S. 325. "God wot", Lucr. 1345 etc.; "sheepcot", As. 2, 4, 84 etc.; "tut an he were", "tut" oft Gent. 2, 3, 46 etc.; "to couch at night", "couch" für "lie", Ado 3, 1, 46 etc.; "all kind of service", Adj. in der Mehrzahl mit Hauptwort in der Einzahl, vgl. "these kind of knaves". Lr. 2, 2, 107; "they had talk" für "converse about", All's 5, 2, 56; "to carol so loud", "loud" für "loudly", Ant. 2, 2, 21 etc.

S. 326. "they had sport", auch Wiv. 2, 1, 204; "these news", Quart ed. H. 4, B. 1, 1, 137 und R. 2 III. 4, 100; "God willing", willing = determining, Ham. 1, 5, 186.

S. 327. "to get to horse", Shr. 4, 3, 193 etc.; "holds her stayed", "stayed" für "detained", Gent. 2, 2, 15 etc.; "never a whit", Tit. 4, 2, 53.

S. 328. "man-beast", vgl. "man-monster", Tp. 3, 2, 14; "entry" für "entrance", Macb. 2, 2, 66; "donned", Ham. 4, 5, 52 etc.; "trenchant steel", vgl. trenchant sword. Tim. 4, 3, 115.

S. 329. „scullion knave", "scullion" als verächtlicher Ausdruck. Ham. 2, 2, 616 etc.; "belike" oft Gent. 1, 2, 85 etc.; "wits" für "understanding", oft Ado 1, 1, 66; "nor shamed to bawl", "shamed" für "was ashamed", öfters Lucr. 1084 etc.; "courtesies", in der Mehrzahl, Ado 4, 1, 322 etc.; "begone", As. 3, 3, 105 etc.; "shrilling" = "crying in a loud voice", vgl. "shrill forth", Troil. 5, 3, 84; "I know thee, ay", "ay" als Verstärkung der Bedeutung, Wint. 2, 1, 138 etc.; "ungentle", im Sinne von "harsh, rude", Err. 4, 2, 21 etc.

S. 330. "have at thee" für "take care", H. 6, B. 2, 3, 92 etc.; "they shocked" = "rush together with violence", John 5, 7, 117; "fellowship" für "companionship, society", Oth. 2, 1, 93 etc. "that by some device"; "that" als "because", Ven. 1062 etc.; "or die therefore", therefore für for it, for that, H. 4, B. 5, 3, 112 etc.; "haling" für "hauling", "from off his neck", "from off" für "off", öfters Mids. 4, 1, 70 etc.

S. 331. "wreaked themselves" für "revenged", Ven. 1004 etc.; "good now", als vollkommener Satz, oft by Sh., Meas. 2, 1, 63 etc.; "a life worth somewhat", "somewhat" für "something", Wiv. 4, 5, 128 etc.; "reward worshipfully", "worshipfully" für "respectably, handsomely", R. 3 III. 4, 41; "harbourage", John. II. 234; "a rout of foresters", "rout" als "gang, set", H. 4, B. 4, 1, 33; "cate", Err. 3, 1, 28 etc.; "part-amazed", vgl. part-created, H. 4, B. 1, 3, 60; "or else the king", else überflüssig, oft bei Sh. Gent. 3, 2, 87; "therewithal", Gentl. 4, 4, 90.

S. 332. "despite of day", despite of, Lucr. 732 etc.; "methinks", oft Gent. 1, 1, 41 etc.; "ruth", Sonn. 132, 4 etc.; "thy much folly", "much" als Adj. nach dem Pronomen Possess, vgl. "thy much misgovernment" Ado 4, 1, 100, "thy much goodness", Meas. V. 534.

S. 333. "I accord it easily", "easily" für "willingly, readily", Cor. 2, 3, 204 etc.; "thou begone", As. 3, 3, 105 etc.

S. 334. "and to boot" für "into the bargain", H. 4, A. 3, 2, 97 etc.; "co-mates", As. 2, 1, 1; as "being all battered", "as being" für "as if", Ven. 630; Sonn. 132, 1 etc.

S. 335. "belike", oft Gent. 1, 2, 85 etc.; "rosemaries and bay" ganz derselbe Ausdruck. Per. 4, 6, 160; "a ward", als district to guard, Meas. 2, 1, 281 etc.

S. 336. "they lighted" für "alighted", Caes. 5, 3, 31 etc.; "foredooming", Lr. 5, 3, 291; "strike vainly" für "ineffectually", LLL 1, 1, 14 etc.; "thy pardon", als vollkommener Satz, oft Tp. 1, 2, 296; "hast mazed my wit", "mazed" für "amazed, perplexed", Mids. 2, 1, 113 etc.; "to cope your quest", "cope" ohne "with" für "encounter", Ven. 888 etc.; "good sooth", als Interjection, oft Mids. 2, 2, 129 etc.

S. 337. "hard at hand", Oth. 2, 1, 268; "suck an allegory", vgl. "suck wisdom", Rom. 1, 3, 68; "out, sword"; "out" used imperatively, Lucr. 1016.

S. 338. "at the last" für "at last", R. 2 III. 2, 169; "rate at her child", "rate at" für "rate", Merch. 3, 2, 260; "good lord" als Anrede H, 6, B. 2, 1, 196, vgl. "good sir" Tp. 1, 2, 88.

S. 339. "Ramp ye lions", vgl. "ramping lion", H. 6, C. 5, 2, 13; "hence" im Sinne von "begone", Ven. 382 etc.; "dream on his liege" für "dream of", öfters in Sh., Meas. 2, 2, 179 etc.; "still reported", still für "constantly, ever", oft, R. 3 I. 3, 146 etc.; "when one might meet", "might" für "should", As. 3, 5, 35 etc.; "with fineness", "fineness" für "ingenuity", Troil. 1, 3, 209.

S. 340. "thunder-gloom", vgl. thunder-like Cor. 1, 4, 59; "in converse" für conversation, Haml. 2, 1, 42 etc.; "the glooming" für "gloom", Rom. 5, 3, 305; "on the marge" für "margin", vgl. sea-marge Tp. 4, 1, 69; "circled" für "encircled", Lucr. 407 etc.; "housed" für "dwelled", Rom. 3, 5, 190; "nightblack", vgl. coalblack", Ven. 533 etc.; "trick thyself" für "dress, adorn", Ham. 2, 2, 479 etc.; "cast to ground" für "to the ground", Tit. 2, 2, 26 etc.; "buffet" H. 4, A. 2, 3, 35 etc.; "throughly" für "thoroughly", Tp. 3, 3, 14 etc.

S. 341. "large mirth", vgl. "be large in mirth", Macb. 3, 4, 11; "stay the world from", "stay from" für "keep back," Merchant 3, 2, 24 etc.

Marriage of Geraint.

S. 341. "fronted him", "front" für "met", H. 4, B. 4, 1, 25 etc.; "service done", "service" Einzahl für Mehrzahl, Per. 5, 1, 255 etc.; "there lived no proof", "lived" für "existed", R. 3 V. 5, 40 etc.; "fair permission", "fair" für "kind, gracious", Merch. 1, 1, 164 etc.; "shores of Severn", "shores" für "banks", Wiv. 3, 5, 15 etc.; "he compassed her" für "encompassed", Troil. 1, 3, 276 etc.

S. 342. "far liefer", vgl. "liefest" H. 6, B. 3, 1, 164; "harness" für "armour", Tim. 1, 2, 53 etc.; "mightful hand" für "powerful", Tit. 4, 4, 5; "I dare to tell", "dare to", Sonn. 26, 13 etc.; "O me", Rom. 4, 5, 19 etc.; "for all my pains", "for" statt "in spite of", oft Ado 2, 1, 57 etc.

S. 343. "he gave order", Einzahl für Mehrzahl, dieser Ausdruck "gave order" Shr. 4, 3, 118 etc.; "covert", Jagdausdruck Wint. 4, 4, 664 etc.; "hound of deepest mouth", "mouth" hier "barking", vgl. "dogs which hath the deeper mouth", H. 6, A. 2, 4, 12; "he lagged latest", "latest" für "last", gewöhnlich bei Sh., Oth. 1, 3, 38 etc.

S. 344. "made answer", oft. Meas. 3, 2, 165 etc.; "I will ask it of himself", "to ask a thing of a person", Gent. 5, 4, 150 etc.; "by my faith", Ausruf, Ado 2, 1, 242 etc.; "She made to the dwarf", "make" für "go, move", Err. 1, 1, 93 etc.; "at losing of the hunt", "losing of", Ant. 2, 1, 8.

S. 345. "flashed into spleen"; "flash into" für "break out", Lr. 1, 3, 4; "nothings", Alls 2, 5, 33 etc.; "can I get me", "get me" reflex, Caes. 2, 4, 37; "scantly", Ant. 3, 4, 6; "spleenful", Tit. 2, 3, 191; "partake the entertainment", "partake" für "partake of" oder "in", Wint. 2, 1, 41; "But in", absol. für "go in", Merch. 2, 2, 165.

S. 346. "turret stair" für stairs, Rom. 2, 4, 201; "by God's rood", vgl. "by the holy rood"; "flesh" für "animal food", Shr. 4, 1, 178 etc.; "right o'er a mount of stones", right = "in a straight line". Compl. 26 etc.

S. 347. "and after went" für afterwards, Lucr. 1522 etc.; "it served for kitchen" für "serve as", Ado 1, 3, 48 etc.; "spread the board", "board" für "table", Cymb. 3, 6, 51 etc.; "he had longing", vgl. "I have longings", Ant. 5, 2, 284; "I pray your courtesy", "pray" mit einem direkten Abstract. Accus., vgl. "I pray your patience" Ado 5, 1, 280, "pray forbearance", Cymb. 2, 5, 10; "grateful is the noise", "grateful" als "pleasant", Troil. 1, 2, 12.

S. 348. "at mine uttermost", Merch. 1, 1, 156 etc.; "howsoever patient", "howsoever" für "although", Meas. 2, 1, 231 etc.

S. 349. "bloodless east", "bloodless" für "pale", Lucr. 1597 etc.; "the East quickens to the Sun", "quickens" für "receive life", Lr. 3, 7, 39 etc.; "in field" für "in the field", LLL. 5, 2, 556; "princelike", Cymb. 5, 5, 293; "it drained their force", "force für forces", Ven. 29 etc.

S. 350. "he bit the bone" (with the sword), vgl. "I have a sword and it shall bite", Wives 2, 1, 136 etc.; "forgave him easily", "easily" für "readily", Gentl. 4, 4, 136 etc.; "it were but little grace" = "it would reflect little credit on", ähnliche Stelle H. 6, A. 2, 1, 79.

S. 351. "a carp was patched", "patched" für "disfigured", John. 3, 1, 47; "birds of sunny plume", "plume" für "plumage", Ven. 314 etc.; "seize on her" für "seize", H. 4, B. 5, 3, 145 etc.; "I trow", Shr. 1, 2, 4 etc.; "look on it" für "look at", Ven. 307 etc.; "scarce divide" für "scarcely", oft, Lucr. 857; "dame Eniol", "dame" statt "lady", oft Lucr. 21 etc.; "he found the sack", "sack" als "plunder", H. 6, A. 2, 2, 15.

S. 352. "flaws", plötzlicher Wind, Ven. 456 etc.; "careful robins", "careful" als "watchful", Tp. 1, 2, 174.

S. 353. "gaudy day", derselbe Ausdruck, H. 6, B. 4, 1, 1 [This is likewise the name for several college festivals at Oxford].

Geraint.

S. 354. "tend upon her" für "wait on, pax attention", All's 3, 2, 84 etc.; "her lord whole"; "whole" als "uninjured" für Personen, Ven. 370 etc.; "the sweet heavens", absol. Haml. 3, 3, 45; auf S. 350 kommt "sweet heaven" in der Einzahl vor, auch im absol. Sinne, bei Shs. Lr. 1, 5, 50. S. 355. "crying to his fellow", "fellow" als "comrade", Tp. 1, 2, 416 etc.; "possess your horse", "possess" = "take possession of", As. 4; 1, 144 etc.; "brace of comrades", "brace" für Personen, oft, vgl. "brace of lords" Tp. V. 126 etc.; „struck home", vgl. "charge home", Cor. 1, 4, 38. S. 356. "stubborn-shafted", vgl. "stubborn-hard", M. Edd John 4, 1, 67; "set on" für "attack", H. 4 A. 5, 2, 97; "tongue-tied" öfters Sonn. 66, 9 etc., "larger-limbed", cp. "good-limbed" H. 4 B. 3, 2, 113.

S. 357. "the pain she had", "pain" für "trouble, effort", R. 3 I. 3, 117 etc.; "disedge", Cymb. 3, 4, 96; 'her government", für "control", Cymb. 2, 4, 150; "stomach" für "appetite", Gent. 1, 2, 68 etc.; "to close with his pleasure", "pleasure" für "humour", H. 4 B. 2, 4, 354 etc.; "in extremity of delight", vgl. "extremity of mishap" Err. 1, 1, 142. S. 358. "moved to laughter", vgl. "moved to passion", LLL. 4, 3, 202, "moved to wrath", Tit. I. 419, "moved to rage", Ant. 2, 5, 70; "daw" für "jackdaws", Ado 2, 3, 264 etc.

S. 359. "your leave", absol. Haml. 1, 2, 51; "sweet civility" für "gentleness", Cymb. 4, 2, 79; "dumbly", Ven. 1059 etc.; "self-pity", vgl. "self-chastity", Oth. 2, 3, 202; "to cross us", "cross" für "disturb, trouble", Gent. 2, 6, 40 etc.; "do not practise on me", für "try to deceive", Ado 2, 1, 38, 2 H. IV. 2, 1, 125; "weary to the death" für "to death", vgl. "hurt to the death", Oth. 2, 3, 163 etc.

S. 360. "stout Prince", „stout" für "proud", Tw. 2, 5, 185 etc.; "overtoiled", vgl. "overstained", John 3, 1, 236 etc.; "to sound on", John 3, 3, 39; "she did him service" für "attendance", Meas. V. 437 etc.; "armours". Mehrzahl, Troil. 5, 3, 46 etc; "amaze" für "amazement", LLL. II. 246. S. 361. "More near", R. 3 IV. 3 49; "motion of the man", "motion" für "movement", Tw. 3, 4, 304.

S. 362. "a loss falls", "fall" für "happen", Merch. 3, 2, 134 etc.; "he was pricked in combat", "pricked" für "wounded", Lucr. 319 etc.; "man-at-arms", H. 6 C. 5, 4, 42; "scour into the coppice", "scour" für "run off", Tim. 5, 2, 15; "ever-fancied", vgl. "ever-esteemed", LLL. 1, 1, 268, "ever-preserved", Haml. 2, 2, 296; "right-honest", vgl. "right-drawn", R. 2 I. 1, 46.

S. 363. "Falling afternoon", vgl. "falling sickness", Caes. 1, 2, 256; "doffed", Shr. 3, 2, 102; "flesh" als "meat", Shr. 4, 1, 178 etc.; "on the sudden" für "on a sudden", Ven. 749 etc. S. 364. "yonder man", "yonder" als Pronomen, oft, Meas. 1, 2, 87 etc.; "cried out upon her talk", im Sinne von "exclaim against", H. 4 A. 4, 3, 81 etc.; "weed" für "clothes", Cor. 2, 3, 329 etc.; "gentlewomen" für "waiting maids of a lady of high rank", Ado 2, 3, 323 etc.

S. 365. "brute Earl", "brute" als Adjv. Ham. 3, 2, 110; "life-long", vgl. "livelong", Macb. 2, 3, 65; "in his mood", "mood" für "anger", Gent. 4, 1, 51 etc.; "dame" im verächtlichen Sinne für "lady", Shr. II. 23; "griefs" für "pain, suffering", Lucr. 139.

S. 366. "lawless hour", "lawless" als "licentious", Gent. 4, 1, 54 etc.; "powers" für "armed forces", John 3, 3, 70 etc. S. 367. "strange chances", "chances" für "fortunes", Cor. 4, 1, 5 etc. S. 368. "brotherlike", H. 6 C. 5, 1, 105; "tendance" für "care, attention", Tim. 1, 1, 57 etc.; "hurt" für "wounds", Cor. 2, 1, 166 etc.

S. 369. "man of men", Ant. 1, 5, 72; "or I or he", "or...
or" statt "either . . . or" kommen bei beiden sehr oft vor.
z. B. S. 370 "or proven or not", S. 371 "or dame or
damsel", S. 378 "or devil or man" etc., vgl. Sonn. 75, 14,
Merch. 1, 1, 150 etc.; "light-winged", Oth. 1, 3, 269, vgl.
"fleet-winged", Lucr. 1216 etc.; "sweet-voiced", Err. V. 418,
vgl. "low-voiced", Ant. 3, 3, 16, "silver-voiced", Per. 5, 1,
111 etc.

Balin and Balan.

S. 369. "realm rendered tributary", vgl. "I render
tributary tears", Ven. 1045; "laugh upon" für "laugh,
at", Shr. 4, 4, 76 etc. S. 370. "pursuivant", H. 6 A. 2,
5, 5 etc. S. 371. "enow", Merch. 3, 5, 24 etc.; "thy
moods" für "bad humour", H. 5 IV. 7, 38. S. 372. "foughten",
H. V. 4, 6, 18; "he hardly scaled", "hardly" für "with difficulty", Gent. 2, 1, 115 etc.; "toothed", Ven. 1117 etc.; "they
approved him", "approve" für "be fond of", Sonn. 42, 3
etc., H. 4 B. 5, 5, 59; "lame-born", vgl. S. 391. "fool-born,
mean-born" etc.

S. 373. "good morrow", öfters, "Ven. 859 etc.;
"quince", Rom. 4, 4, 2; "high-set", vgl. "firm-set", Macb.
2, 1, 56; "sad-set", Lucr. 1662 etc.; "close-bowered", vgl.
"close-tongued", Lucr. 770 etc. S. 374. "whereout", Troil.
4, 5, 245; "deep-hued", vgl. "deep-brained", Compl. 209,
"deep-mouthed", John 5, 2, 173, "deep-searched", LLL. 1,
1, 85 etc.

S. 375. "lichen-bearded", vgl. "white-bearded",
Ado 2, 3, 124, "scarce-bearded", Ant. 1, 1, 21; "ivy-tods",
"tod" seltenes Wort, Wint. 4, 3, 34; "crown-royal", vgl.
"crown-imperial", Wint. 4, 4, 126; "bossed" für "embossed",
Shr. II. 355; "massiest", "massy" für "massive", Tp. 3, 3,
67 etc.; "passing gentle", "passing" für "exceedingly",
oft, Ven. 297 etc.; "to mouth a foulness", "mouth" als
Zeitwort, Haml. 3, 2, 3 etc.; "felon-talk", vgl. "table-talk",
Merch. 3, 5, 93.

S. 376. "music was dumbed", "dumb" als Verbum, 2 mal, Ant. 1, 5, 50 etc.; "damsel-errant", vgl. "sheknight-errant", H. 4 B. 5, 4, 25; "the wold" in der Einzahl, Lor. 3, 4, 125; "scarce spy", "scarce" als Adverbium oft Merch. 2, 1, 5 etc.; "mocking-wise", vgl. "burden-wise", Lucr. 1133 etc. S. 377. "thou art bounden", "bounden" 2 mal As. 1, 2, 298; "maws"; Ven. 602 etc. S. 378. "vestal knighthood", vgl. "vestal livery", Rom. 2, 2, 8, "vestal modest", Rom. 3, 3, 38; "the told-of", vgl. "never-heard-of", Tit. 2, 3, 285; "mark me well", vgl. "mark it well", Meas. 2, 1, 158, "mark me", Gent. 4, 4, 39.

S. 379. "foulness" für "wickedness", Ado. 4, 1, 155 etc.; "cradle-time", vgl. "leaping-time (time of youth)", Cymb. 4, 2, 200 etc.; "Sir Boy, Sir Chick", diese Art von Anrede mit "Sir" ist sehr beliebt von beiden", vgl. "Sir knight", H. 5 II. 2, 67, "Sir Knave", Err. 1, 2, 72, "Sir Boy", Ado. 5, 1, 83, "Sir Page", Wint. 1, 2, 135 etc.; "brokenly", ungebräuchliches Adverbium, H. V. 5, 2, 106.

Merlin and Vivien.

"virgin knight", Ado. 5, 3, 13; "virgin" als Adjv. kommt bei Sh. sehr oft vor "virgin hand", Sonn. 154, 8; "limit of bond", vgl. "limit of embassy", John I. 22.

S. 381. "innocency" für "innocence", Meas. 3, 2, 10 etc.; "a-hawking", vgl. "a-mending", Lucr. 452, "a-mending", Troil. 1, 3, 159; "the while", Merch. 2, 1, 31 etc.; "give him the lie", Mids. 3, 1, 138 etc.; "fear-tremulous", vgl. "fear-surprised", Ham. 1, 2, 203.

S. 382. "supersensual", vgl. "supersubtle", Oth. 1, 3, 363, "superfinical", Lr. 2, 2, 19, "superdainty", Shr. II. 189 etc.; the three following hawking expressions are also found, "jesses", Oth. 3, 3, 261, "leash", Wint. 4, 4, 477, "Cure" Hauptwort, Shr. 4, 1, 195 etc.; "stranger woman", vgl. "stranger queen", LLL. 4, 2, 143.

S. 383. "greeted fair", Adj. für Adv. im Sinne von "kindly", Err. 3, 2, 11; "sprightly talk", All's 2, 1. 78 etc. "the which", "which" mit bestimmten Artikeln oft Wiv. 2,

2, 84 etc. S. 384. "gleams of March", "gleams" nicht mehr gebräuchlich in diesem Sinne vgl. Mids. V. 279; "answered quick", "quick" als Adv. oft, Meas. 4, 1, 7 etc.; "eyeless", Rom. 5, 3, 126 etc. S. 387. "counterchange", Cymb. 5, 5, 396; "trumpetblowings", vgl. "trumpet-clangor", H. 4 B. 5, 5, 42 etc. S. 387. "disfame", unusual compound, vgl. "distemperance", Per. 5, 1, 27, "distemperature", Err. V. 82 etc.

S. 388. "graff", Lucr. 1062 etc. "misfaith", ungebräuchlich, vgl. "misdoubt", H. 4 B. 4, 1, 206 etc. S. 389. "good man" als "husband", Shr. Ind. 2, 107. S. 390. "made proffer", All's 2, 1, 150 etc.; "whelm" für "overwhelm", Wiv. 2, 2, 143. "in a wild", Einzahl für Mehrzahl, vgl. "the wild of Kent", H. 4 A. 2, 1, 60; "nor . . . nor" statt neither . . . nor", Sonn. V. 12 etc.; "glassy-headed", vgl. "beetle-headed", Shr. 4, 1, 161, "puppy-headed", Tp. 2, 2, 159, "sleek-headed", Caes. 1, 2, 193 etc.; "writ" für "written", Ado. 2, 3, 138 etc.

S. 391. "careless" für "heedless", Ven. 556 etc.; "loathly plume", für "loathful", Tp. IV. 20; "full-fed", Lucr. 694; "many-corridored", vgl. "many-headed", Cor. 2, 3, 58; "spleen-born", H. 4 B. 5, 5, 59, vgl. "fool-born, mean-born", H. 6 B. 3, 1, 335 etc. S. 392. "glimmered chastely", "chastely" seltenes Adverbium. All's 1, 3, 218 etc.; "flustered with wine", "flustered" für "heated", Oth. 2, 3, 60.

S. 393. "hoary fell", "fell" für "skin", As. 3, 2, 55 etc.; "in a wink", "moment", Cymb. 3, 4, 103 etc.; "crueller", irregular comparative, Cor. 5, 2, 71; "part heard" für "partly", vgl. "part confessed", Oth. 5, 2, 296; "bare-gnawing", vgl. "bare-gnawn", Lr. 5, 3, 122, "bare-ribbed", John 5, 2, 177. S. 394. "seeming-injured", vgl. "seeming-virtuous", Ham. 1, 5, 46; "to sleek" = "to make smooth", Mcb. 3, 2, 27. S. 395. "white-listed", vgl. "white-limed", Tit. 4, 2, 98, "white-handed", LLL. 5, 2, 220 etc.

Lancelot and Elaine.

S. 395. "soilure", Troil. 4, 1, 56; "tinct", a dye, Haml. 3, 4, 91 etc. S. 396. "God's mercy", als Ausruf, All's 1, 3, 155. S. 397. "Sir King", Tp. V. 106; "ancient wound", vgl. Tp. 2, 1, 286; "allowed of all men", "of" statt "by", nach allow. Wint. 4, 1, 29. S. 398. "to speak true", Tp. 2, 1, 20 etc.; "wordless", Lucr. 112; "barren-beaten", vgl. "barren-spirited", Caes. 4, 1, 36. S. 399. "lustihood" für "lustiness", Ado 5, 1, 76 etc.; "lineaments" für "features", Merch. 3, 4, 15 etc. S. 400. "kindly man", "kindly" für "kind", vor Personen vgl. "kindly creature", Ant. 2, 5, 78; "answered at full" für "in full", vgl. "dilate at full", Err. 1, 1, 123; "we live apart", d. h. "at a distance away from the world", Tit. 5, 1, 112 etc.

S. 401. "make cheer", H. 4 B. 5, 3, 18; "from out the town", für "out of", John 5, 2, 136; "do me this grace" für "favour", Err. 2, 1, 87 etc. S. 402. "instant reverance", "instant" für "immediate", All's 2, 4, 49 etc.; "nameless king", wörtlich "without a name", nicht gebräuchlich, Lucr. 522 etc.; "youth now crescent", "crescent" als Ajdv. für "increasing", Ham. 1, 3, 11 etc. S. 403. "stranger knight", "stranger" als Adjv., Per. 2, 3, 67 etc.; "and helms" für "steer", Meas. 3, 2, 151; "holpen", Tp. 1, 2, 63 etc. S. 404. "fled the lists", vgl. fled the field", H. 4 B. 1, 1, 18; "sore wounded", vgl. "sore hurt", Troil. 5, 5, 14; "such an one", Macb. 4, 3, 66 etc.

S. 405. "tarriance", Gent. 2, 7, 90 etc.; "wearied of the quest", "of" für "with", Ven. 853 etc.; "unhearing", ungebräuchlich, vgl. "unseeing", Sonn. 43, 8, "unaching", Cor. 2, 2, 152; "parted from the jousts" für "departed", Gent. 1, 1, 71 etc. S. 406. "the Prince accorded with", ungebräuchlich für "agreed", H. 6 B. 3, 1, 269 etc.; "by mine head", Ausruf, vgl. "by my head", Rom. 3, 1, 38 etc.; "brethren" für "brothers", As. 2, 1, 67 etc.

S. 408. "I must hence", "hence" mit Hilfszeitwort allein, vgl. "let us hence", Ado 5, 3, 30; "you shall hence", Merch. 3, 2, 313; "latest word", "latest" für "last", "latest words", Troil. 1, 3, 33. S. 409. "feverous" für "feverish", Troil. 3, 2, 38 etc.; "uncourteous" für "discourteous", Tw. V. 369; "the simples" für "medical herbs", Wiv. 1, 4, 65; "fine care", "fine" für "delicate, tender", Tw. 1, 1, 33 etc.

S. 410. "a deadly hurt" für "mortal", Err. V. 70. S. 412. "a goodmorrow", Ven. 859 etc.; "yesternight", oft, Ado. 4, 1, 84 etc.; "loveless", Pilg. 216. S. 413. "Muse at me", Macb. 3, 4, 85; "look on this man" für "look at", Caes. 1, 2, 87 etc.; "discomfort" für "sorrow", Macb. 4, 2, 29 etc.; "shrive me clean", Merch. 1, 2, 144; "ghostly man" für "Priester", Meas. 4, 3, 51. S. 414. "palled in samite", "palled" für "enveloped", "wrapped", Macb. 1, 5, 52; "creature" für "servant", Tim. 1, 1, 116 etc.; "oared", als Verbum Tp. 2, 1, 118.

S. 415. "she shines me down", "shine down" für "outshine", vgl. "French shone down English", H. 8. I. 4, 60. S. 416. "tongueless", R. 2 I. 1, 105; "my lord liege", vgl. "my sovereign liege", R. 2 I. 1, 129; "to estate them", "estate" als Zeitwort, Tp. 4, 85 etc. S. 417. "I have affiance", "affiance" für "confidence", Cymb. 1, 6, 163; "heirless", Wint. 5, 1, 10; "it is worthy love" statt "worthy of", Gent. 1, 2, 6 etc.; "courtesies" in der Mehrzahl, Meas. V. 15.

Holy Grail.

S. 419. "world-old", vgl. "world-wearied", Rom. 5, 3, 112, "wit-old", LLL. 5, 1, 66; "days of yore", Sonn. 68, 14. S. 420. "gave herself to fast" statt "to fasting", Lucr. 891 etc.; "it is not his use to hunt", "use" für "custom", Meas. 3, 2, 134 etc.; "dubbed him knight", H. 4 B. 5, 3, 78 etc.; "prayed to the uttermost", vgl. Shr. 4, 3, 80. S. 421. "shore away that wealth of hair", "shear" gebraucht für Personen, vgl. "the golden tresses

were shorn away", Sonn. 68, 6. S. 422. "scaped", oft für
"escaped", Tp. 2, 2, 117; "crying on help" für "out for",
Oth. 5, 1, 48 etc.; "pray Heaven", als vollendeter Satz,
vgl. Gent. 2, 7, 79 etc.
 S. 423. "heads of violence", "heads" für "armed
forces", John 5, 2, 113. S. 424. "to see the like", H. 6
A. 1, 2, 22, vgl. "hear the like", Wiv. 2, 1, 70. S. 425.
"lowly vale", "lowly" im physischen Sinne als Adjv. R. 2
II. 4. 21. S. 426. "sacring of the mass", vgl. "sacring
bell", H. 8. III. 2, 295. S. 427. "deathful", H. 6 B. 3, 2,
404; "in sooth", viel von den Dramatikern gebraucht, Wiv.
3, 4, 110 etc., "ills" für "illnesses", Lucr. 656; "burdock",
Lr. 4, 4, 4; "I made thither", "made" für "go", Wint. 4,
4, 554 etc.
 S. 428. "but O the pity", im absolutem Sinne, vgl.
"the pity of it", Oth. 4, 1, 206; "made joy", John 3,
4, 107. S. 429. "O grace to me", vgl. Troil. 3, 1, 16;
"mighty reverent", "mighty" als Adverbium, Wiv. 3, 3, 221.
S. 431. "boat shock earth", vgl. John 5, 7, 117. S. 432.
"boldened" für "emboldened", As. 2, 7, 91 etc.

Pelleas.

 S. 433. "knightly sword", R. 2 IV. 29. S. 434. "lip
the marge", "lip" als Verbum, Oth. 4, 1, 72, "richly trapt"
für "dressed", Tim. 1, 2, 189. S. 435. "holden" für "held",
H. 6 B. 2, 4, 71. S. 436. "unsunny", vgl. "unsunned",
Cymb. 2, 5, 13, "bide Sir Baby", "bide" für "bear, endure",
Sonn. 58, 7 etc.; "fly us" für "fly from", Mids. 2, 1, 240
etc.; "small matter"! vgl. "No matter!" Sonn. 44, 5 etc.;
"hest" für "order", Tp. 1, 2, 274 etc. S. 437. "light on
words", "light on" für "find", vgl. Ado 2, 1, 34; "For pity
of", Ven. 577 etc.; "weakling", Lucr. 584.
 S. 438. "forsworn" für "perjured", Meas. 4, 1, 2;
"out of door" für "doors", LLL. III. 92; "to thrall",
seltenes Verbum, Shr. 1, 1, 225; "handless", Troil. 5, 5,
34 etc. S. 439. "winded the bugle", "wind" für "blow",
Ado 1, 1, 243; "avaunt", dramatischer Ausdruck, Wiv. 1,

3, 90 etc., etc.; "Ay, Ay" für "yes", oft, Tp. 1, 2, 268 etc.; "cried upon your name", "cry upon", As. 4, 3, 150; "Pity on him", Tw. 2, 5, 14 etc. S. 440. "inmost sleep", "inmost" für "deepest", Tit. 4, 3, 12. S. 442. "mazed" für "amazed", Mids. 2, 1, 113 etc.; "overrode him" für "rode over", H. 4 B. 1, 1, 30; "disedge", Cymp. 3, 4, 96.

Last Tournament.

S. 443. "carcenet", Sonn. 52, 8 etc.; "unscarred from beak", "from" für "by", R. 3 IV. 4, 209 etc. S. 444. "he sware me to a message", "sware" im Sinne von "to cause to take an oath", LLL. 1, 1, 69, S. 445. "tend curiously" für "carefully", Ado, 5, 1, 157 etc.; "otherwhere", Err. 2, 1, 30 etc.; "by deeds to be at one with vows", "at one with", H. V. 5, 2, 204; "bygone Merlin", "bygone" als Adjv. vor einer Person, Wint. 1, 2, 32 etc. S. 446. "vailed his eyes", vgl. "vailed his eyelids", Ven. 966.

S. 447. "pettish", Troil. 2, 3, 139; "langhed shrilly", "shrilly" als Adv. Tit. 2, 3, 18; "Autumn-tide", vgl. "Lammas-tide", Rom. 1, 3, 15, "Shrove-tide" H. 4 B. 5, 3, 38; "a catch" für "song", Tp. 3, 2, 126 etc.; "twangled on his harp", "twangle" für "twang", vgl. "twangler", Shr. II. 159.

S. 448. "damosel", "damosell", Ff. LLL. 1, 1, 292; "spat a pish", "pish", Oth. 2, 1, 270 etc.; "a naked aught"; "naked" für "mere, simple", vgl. "a naked name", Gent. 2, 4, 142; "mincing with his feet", vgl. "mincing steps", Merch. 3, 4, 67.

S. 449. "Tuwhoo", vgl. "tu-who", LLL. 5, 2, 923 etc.; "a drift of foliage", vgl. "drift of bullets", John II. 412. S. 450. "whereout", Troil. 4, 5, 245; "blood-red", vgl. "fiery-red", Mids. 3, 2, 391, "wax-red", Ven. 516; "darkling", Mids. 2, 2, 86 etc. S. 451. "in dead night", vgl. "in dead midnight", Sonn. 43, 11 etc.; "catlike", As. 4, 3, 116. S. 452. "dole of beauty", vgl. "dole of honour", All's 2, 3, 176.

S. 453. "the king was fulfilled with" für "fill with", Lucr. 1258; "in utter dark" für "darkness", oft, Sonn. 43, 4; "leman", Wiv. 4, 2, 172 etc.; "malkin", Cor. 2, 1, 224 etc. S. 454. "unswear", seltenes Verbum, Oth. 4, 1, 31 etc.; "throned in hall", "throned" für "enthroned", Cor. 5, 4, 26 etc.; "hillsnow", vgl. "mountainsnow", Ven. 750; "elsewise", vgl. in demselben Sinne "otherwise", Tp. 2, 1, 128. S. 455. "thy saw" für "say, maxim", Lucr. 244 etc ; "dews", seltene Mehrzahl, Cor. 2, 3, 35 etc.

Guinevere.

S. 456. "he couched" für "lay hidden", Wiv. 5, 2, 1 etc.; "holp", Cor. 5, 3, 63 etc.; "green-suited", vgl. "sober-suited", Rom. 3, 2, 11 etc. S. 457. "to front in hall", "front" als "face, meet", Ant. 1, 4, 79 etc.; "farewells", seltene Mehrzahl, Troil. 4, 4, 46 etc.; "lionlike", vgl. "bearlike", Mcb. 5, 7, 2, "dragonlike", Cor. 4, 7, 23 etc.

S. 458. "weald", H. 4 A. 2, 1, 60; "that foreruns the morn", "forerun" seltenes Verbum, Rom. 5, 1, 53 etc.; "folk" Einzahl selten, Haml. 5, 1, 30; "they spared to ask", "spared" für "forbear", Tp. 2, 1, 25 etc.; "housel", vgl. "unhouseled", Haml. 1, 5, 77 ; "if ye list", vgl. "if you list", Tp. 3, 2, 19 etc.

S. 459. "prate", als Hauptwort für "prating", John 4, 1, 25 etc. S. 460. "at evenings", vgl. "a mornings". Ado. 3, 2, 42 etc., "a nights", Tw. 1, 3, 5 etc. S. 461, "they set her on" für "incite", Meas. V. 112 etc.; "gather heart", vgl. "gather patience", Ado 5, 1, 19. S. 463. "scathe", Tit. 5, 1, 7 etc.; "the wonted number", "wonted" als Adjv., Ven. 1053 etc.: "on the stair", "stair", Einzahl see S. 346. S. 464. "urge his crimes", "urge" für "speak of", Caes. 2, 1, 155 etc. S. 465. "fume of hearts", "fume" für "anger", Ven. 316 etc. S. 466. "warring senses", vgl. "warring winds", Lr. 4, 7, 32; "almsdeed" für "almsdeeds", H. 6 C. 5, 5, 79.

Passing of Arthur.

S. 467. "in winter of his age", "winter" als Bezeichnung des Alters, Ven. 802 etc.; "Hail, King", oft bei
den Dramatikern, Tp. 1, 2, 189 etc.; "O me, my King",
Ausruf, John I. 220 etc. S. 468. "They know thee for"
für "know thee to be" oder "know thee as", Wint. 2, 2,
297 etc.; "strike the stroke", Ant. 1, 14, 91 etc.;
"bound of Lyonnesse", Einzahl für Mehrzahl, H. 4 A. 4,
1, 51; "deathwhite", vgl. milkwhite", Pilgr. 119, "silver-
white", Lucr. 1405 etc. S. 470. "sleep a sleep", R. 3
V. 3, 164; "helm" für "helmet", öfters, All's 3, 3, 7;
"aidless", Cor. 2, 2, 116.

S. 471. "in the deeps", "deeps" für "ocean, sea",
Gent. 3, 2, 81 etc.; "traitor-hearted", vgl. "shallow-hearted",
Tit. 4, 2, 97, "hollow-hearted", R. 3 IV. 4, 435, "pale-
hearted", Mcb. 4, 1, 85 etc. S. 473. "cuisses", öfters H.
4 A. 4, 1, 105 etc.

Im Anschluss an die vorhergehenden vergleichenden
Zusammenstellungen werden einige allgemeine Bemerkungen
über die verschiedenen Wortklassen angebracht sein.

Artikel. In Tennysons Idylle wird sowohl der be-
stimmte als der unbestimmte Artikel ausgelassen, wie
andererseits der erstere oft pleonastisch steht. Die Beispiele hierfür, die ich gesammelt hatte, sind zu zahlreich, um
sie anzuführen. Ähnliche Beispiele finden sich übrigens
auch bei Shakspere, Spenser und Chaucer. An für a begegnet man hier und da, z. B. S. 356 an hundred; vgl.
Shaks. LLL. 4, 2, 63 "an hundred"; Tp. 1, 2, 30 "an
hair" etc. Spens. F. Q. Bk. I. S. 4 "an hideous", S. 44
"an heap" etc. Chauc. K. T. S. 49 "an hat". Einmal
treffen wir a mit einem Plural verbunden; "a jousts", S.
444; vgl. Malory Bk. II ch 1 "a grete jousts" (die Quelle
des Ausdrucks), Shaks. "a friends" All's 1, 3, 42, ("a

little ways" sagt man noch heute in einigen Gegenden Englands). Spens. F. F. Bk. 2, S. 34 "a thousand grone"; Chauc. K. T. S. 59 "a listes"; auch Malory Bk. 16 ch. 9, "a ten knights".

Hauptwort. Bei den Substantiven ist besonders die Eigentümlichkeit zu beobachten, dass viele in einem Sinne gebraucht sind, den sie sonst nur in der Zeit Shaksperes und Spensers haben z. B. wit für judgment, wits für senses. doom für judgment, flesh für meat, griefs für pain, weed für clothes, powers für armed forces, intent für intention, force für strength etc. Eine grosse Zahl finden wir bei Spenser z. B. F. Q. Bk. 1, S. 1 und 10, weedes für clothes, S. 4 und 78 leman, S. 6 und 135 boughtes (Ausdruck der Wappenkunde), S. 13, 73, 67 etc. intent, assay als Hauptwort, S. 24, 28 hew als Gesichtsfarbe, S. 28 commandment für command, S. 36, 91 brand für sword, S. 38 ensample, S. 53 ruth, S. 61 thralls, S. 67 annoy für annoyance, S. 79 paynim, S. 50 meates and drinkes. In Buch II finden wir S. 45 forces = strength, S. 56 marge = margin, S. 140 pupillage, S. 147 payne = difficulty, S. 155 travell = difficulty. Auch Malory bietet exceptionelle Worte, die sich bei Tennyson wiederfinden z. B. battle = army Bk. 1, ch. 3, 14, 15 etc., in Bk. 1. ch. 9 ordinance = order; Bk. 1, ch. 12, hardy = bold; Bk. 2 ch. 1; avail = advantage; Bk. 4, ch. 2, avow = avowal; Bk. 4, ch. 28, siege = seat; Bk. 15, ch. 7, flesh = meat; Bk. 15, ch. 9, harbourage = shelter; Bk. 19, ch. 2, maying; Bk. 21, ch. 4, harness = armour; ebenso solche Worte wie intent, helm, leman, meates und drinkes, fellowship für companionship etc. Einige dieser Ausdrücke finden sich auch bei Chaucer, z. B. Prol. S. 14 hewe = colour of face; S. 6 flesh = meat; S. 2 felawship; K. I. S. 33 rewthe (ruth), S. 36 harness, S. 36 wede (clothes), S. 36 entente etc. Tennyson bildet sehr häufig Composita mit den Silben -hood und -ling, z. B. S. 327 youthhood, S. 343 queenhood, S. 391 fatherhood,

S. 309 kinglihood, S. 314 changeling, S. 391 reckling, S. 394 cageling, S. 343 weakling etc. Auch Shakspere hat eine grosse Vorliebe für solche Compositionen, vgl. dearling Oth. 1, 2, 68, heartling Wiv. 3, 4, 59, fondling Ven. 229 etc.

Adjektiv. Bemerkenswerth ist hier vor allem die Bildung vieler sonst nicht üblicher Composita auf -less, -like und -ful. Solche auf -less sind z. B. S. 340 fleshless, S. 358 dinnerless, S. 370 kingless, Christlsss, S. 384 eycless, S. 390 hairless, S. 391 proofless, S. 398 wordless, S. 402 bushless, S. 413 peerless, S. 410 tongueless, S. 430 hornless, S. 437 handless, S. 473 companionless; auf -like S. 336 unknightlike, S. 349 princelike, S. 353 sunlike, S. 357 gemlike, S. 368 brotherlike, S. 389 magnetlike, S. 422 dreamlike etc.; auf -ful S. 317 showerful, S. 319 easeful, S. 322 manful, S. 367 prideful, S. 385 presageful, S. 418 noiseful, gustful, S. 424 deathful, S. 453 prayerful. Dergleichen Wörter von exceptioneller Bildung hat Shakspere in Menge, und wir dürfen daher annehmen, dass er in dieser Hinsicht auf Tennyson Einfluss übte, vgl. auf -less dateless Sonn. 30, 6; airless Caes. 1, 3, 94; finless H. 4 A. 3, 1, 151; makeless Sonn. 9, 4; aweless John I. 266; termless, issueless Sonn. 9, 3; chaffless Cymb. 1, 6, 178; wenchless, graveless, stingless etc. etc.; auf -like goddesslike Cymb. 3, 2, 8; cowardlike Lucr. 231; mermaidlike Ham. 4, 7, 177; monsterlike Ant. 4, 12, 36; unknightlike Cymb. 3, 5, 7; dragonlike Cor. 4, 7, 23; mistlike, infantlike, fishlike, heartlike etc.; auf -ful deathful H. 6 B. 3, 2, 404; mistful H. 5, IV. 6, 34; mightful Tit. 4, 4, 5; crimeful, faultful, fraudful, increaseful, offenceful etc.

Verbum. Die Haupteigentümlichkeit, die wir beim Verbum finden, ist der Gebrauch der alten Formen für den Indikativ und das Participium Praeteritum, z. B. S. 309 drave, S. 311 holp, S. 318 clomb, S. 320 clod, S. 333 brake, S. 356 spake, S. 333 drave, S. 339 tare, S. 355 bare, S. 380 sware, S. 395 clave, S. 310 proven, foughten, S. 311 holpen, S. 312 holden, graven, S. 324 carven, S. 337 baken, S. 357

laden, S. 377 bounden, S. 409 writhen, S. 391 wreathen,
S. 423 unproven etc.

Hier scheint Tennyson von Spenser und Malory beeinflusst worden zu sein. Die älteren Imperfektformen finden
sich häufig bei Spenser, ebenso solche Formen, wie rapt
für rapped, dipt für dipped, snapt etc. die Tennyson durch-
gehends gebraucht; vgl. Spens. Bk. I. F. Q. S. 19 bad,
S. 30 sware, bare, S. 118 writ, S. 127 clomb, S. 52 stricken
etc.; vgl. Malory Bk. 1, ch. 6 und 10, holden, ch. 8 gotten,
ch. 22 foughten; Bk. 16, ch. 6 shoven, arriven, Bk. 16
ch. 8 abidden, Bk. 19, ch. 10 yielden, Bk. 20, ch. 13 holpen,
Bk. 21, ch. 6 graven etc. Andere Verba erscheinen z. B.
Spens. F. Q. to rew (rue) S. 20; S. 36 reft; scape für es-
cape und upbrought S. 116. Der Ausdruck "to be ware"
für "aware" findet sich sowohl bei Malory als bei Chaucer
z. B. Mal. Bk. 2, ch. 5, Bk. III ch. 9 etc. Chaucer K. T.
S. 32, 43 etc. Viele ähnliche Ausdrücke haben Malory und
Spenser, z. B. Mal. Bk. I, ch. 1 made cheer, ch. 3 made
affiance, ch. 3 made sorrow, ch. 4 made moan, Bk. 2, ch. 10
I desire you of your courtesy, Bk. 10, ch. 15 let him be:
Spenser Bk. I. F. Q. S. 131 pricked with courage, S. 137
couched his speare, S. 139 unlace his helmet etc.

Adverbium. Zu bemerken ist hier besonders der un-
übliche Comparativ auf -lier, der Gebrauch von full and
right für very zur Bezeichnung des Superlativs; gelegent-
lich findet sich passing und wondrous in gleicher
Funktion. Unregelmässig gebildete Comparative sind z. B.
S. 336 stronglier, S. 356 slowlier, S. 366 plainlier, S. 370
gladlier, S. 371 strictlier, S. 373 fierier, S. 378 unearthlier,
S. 383 kindlier, S. 383 closelier, S. 399 safelier etc. Ge-
legentlich, aber im allgemeinen selten, findet man solche
Formen bei Shakspere z. B. kindlier Pp. V, 24, goodlier
Pp. 1, 2, 483. Full and right, zur Bezeichnung des
Superlativs sind häufig: S. 389 full many, S. 398 full often,
S. 409 full lowly, S. 410 full ill, S. 422 full quickly, S. 433
full fain etc. etc.; S. 398 right fain, S. 408 right fair, S. 361

right honest etc.; S. 375 passing gentle, S. 385 passing wrathful, S. 439 wondrous fair etc. etc. Tennyson scheint hierin ganz Spenser, Malory und Shakspere gefolgt zu sein; vgl. Spens. Bk. I F. Q. S. 3 full jolly, S. 9 full deadly, S. 15 full envious, S. 17 full large etc. etc., S. 3 right faithful, S. 11 right well, S. 41 right glad, S. 43 right fitly etc.; S. 40 wondrous fair, S. 44 wondrous glad, S. 84 wondrous great etc,. etc.; Mal. Bk. 2, ch. 4 full true, Bk. 2, ch. 4 full simple, Bk. 3, ch. 1 full well, Bk. 3, ch. 3 full womanly etc. etc., Bk. 1, ch. 17 right pensive, Bk. 1. ch. 18 right wise etc., Bk. 1, ch. 1 passing good, passing wise, ch. 2 passing fair etc. etc. Lightly für "quickly" kommt öfters bei Tennyson vor, z. B. S. 408, S. 370 etc., vgl. Spenser F. Q. B. I, S. 89, S. 91 etc. Malory Bk. I, ch. 14 etc. öfters.

Präpositionen. Wir haben dieselben schon berührt und entsprechende Fälle aus Shakspere citirt. Bei Spenser und Malory begegnen wir derartigen Unregelmässigkeiten gleichfalls nicht selten. Of für by gebraucht T. oft, z. B. S. 338 "fooled of others", S. 346 "beloved of men", S. 400 "loved of, S. 382 "forgotten of the queen" etc., vgl. Spens. F. Q. Bk. I, S. 9 "accurst of heaven", S. 23 "loved of ladies", S. 42 "drawn of peacocks", S. 62 "scorned of God" etc etc. In Malory haben wir Bk. 1, ch. 1 sick for (für through) anger, ch. 3 how he came to (für by) the sword, ch. 7 departed with (für in) wrath.

Conjunctionen. Sie zeigen nichts Besonderes in ihrem Gebrauche, nor . . . nor für neither . . . nor, or . . . or für either . . . or, kommen oft bei Tennyson vor; aber solchen Unregelmässigkeiten begegnen wir oft bei Shakspere, Spenser und Malory. Der häufige Gebrauch von an für if, und so für if, provided that, wurde schon erwähnt.

Auf den Gebrauch des Wortes All mag noch hingewiesen werden, da er der eigentümlichen Verwendung des Wortes bei Spenser entspricht. Fast auf jeder Seite trifft man all in einem exceptionellen Sinne. Es bedeutet "quite, whole, entirely, everything, altogether und every

possible". Wir lassen einige Beispiele folgen. Ten. S. 312
"all before his time, all as soon as born", S. 321 "all
unwilling", S. 322 "all in fear", S. 325 "all for glory",
S. 330 "smellest all of the kitchen", S. 334 "all as good",
S. 353 "with all welcome, all the threshold", S. 355 "burnt
him all within", S. 357 "I have eaten all", S. 358 "with
all ease", S. 364 "all red" etc. etc. Vgl. Spens. F. Q.
Bk. I. S. 7 "all suddenly", S. 9 "all with fear", S. 17 "all
alarmed", S. 26 "all for pity", S. 81 "all as the dwarf",
S. 82 "horrid all with gold", S. 101 "all so soone", S. 114
"all her place" etc. etc.

Auch das Kunstmittel der **Alliteration** hat Tennyson
in den Idylls angewandt, und zwar ebenso die Vers-Allitteration
wie die Allitteration zweier eng verbundener Wörter.
Und hierin hat er zweifellos wieder Spenser zum Vorbild
gehabt. Jede Seite strotzt von Beispielen; so
finden wir **s**pike **t**hat **s**plit, **w**edded **w**ith **w**insome **w**ife,
knighted from **k**neeling, **c**lang **b**attle axe **c**lash **b**rand,
fight **f**or our **f**air **f**athers, **r**ide about **r**edressing human
wrong, **p**laced a **p**eacock in his **p**ride, **s**trikest a **s**trong
stroke, etc. etc. Die Allitteration zweier eng verbundener
Wörter begegnet man unzählige Male, wie bei Spenser, z. B.
Ten. S. 309 **w**et **w**oods, S. 310 **p**itched **p**avilions, S. 313 **h**oly
hymns, S. 314 **d**reary **d**eeps, S. 317 **h**eathen **h**ordes, S. 320
princely-**p**roud, S. 324 **l**iege-**l**ord, S. 326 **m**ellow **m**aster,
S. 327 **f**oolish **f**ashion, S. 33 **w**an **w**ater, **c**ostly **c**ate, S. 330
gloomy **g**laded, S. 333 **l**oftier **l**ineage, S. 335 **p**leasant **p**resence,
may **m**usic, **s**weet **s**unworship, **r**ose-**r**ed, **d**eep-**d**impled etc.
etc., vgl. Spens. F. Q. Bk. I. S. 1 **w**eak **w**it, S. 2 **d**earest
dread, S. 3 **l**ovely **l**ady, S. 4 **l**emans **l**ap, S. 5 **d**iverse **d**oubt,
S. 10 **l**outing **l**ow, S. 14 **d**iverse **d**ream, S. 20 **s**ad **s**owle,
S. 26 **f**ast **f**ealty, S. 27 **l**yon **l**ord etc. etc.

Das Wort a d o w n, dass bei Ten. öfters vorkommt,
wird oft bei Spens. gebraucht, z. B. F. Q. Bk. I, S. 17, 73,
80 etc.; Ten. S. 395.

Die berühmte Stelle in "The Marriage of Geraint", S. 342, wo fünf aufeinanderfolgende Zeilen mit "Forgetful of" beginnen, scheint auch wieder den Einfluss Spensers anzudeuten; denn wir finden den Ausdruck oft bei ihm, z. B. F. Q. Bk. I, S. 18 Forgetful of the victory, S. 27 Forgetful of his hungry rage, S. 55 Forgetful of his own, S. 62 Forgetful of their yoke etc.

Den Gebrauch von let in folgender Stelle, Ten. S. 310, "the long-lanced battle let their horses run" hat T. ohne Zweifel von Malory herübergenommen, der let häufig so anwendet, z. B. Mal. Bk. I, ch. 13 derselbe Ausdruck; Bk. I, ch. 8 let crye a grete Juste; Bk. 2, ch. 1 let make a cry etc.

Zu den Ausdrücken (Ten. S. 403) "diamond me no diamonds", "prize me no prizes", stellen sich als Parallelen aus Shakspere Rich. II. 2, 3, 87 "grace me no graces, nor uncle me no uncles"; Rom. 3, 5, 153 "Thank me no thankings, nor proud me no prouds".

Verschiedene Ausdrücke erscheinen sowohl in der Bibel als bei Shaks. z. B. often und frequent als Averbien, stay their hands, harness für armour, flesh and wine, victual, cleave to a person, latter für latter part, dream a dream, commune with a person, plucked asnnder, otherwhere etc.

Die Resultate meiner Untersuchung neben den Beziehungen zwischen Tennyson und Malory gedenke ich demnächst an anderer Stelle zu veröffentlichen.

Errata.

S. 6, Z. 31 lies das für dass; S. 11, Z. 9 dem für den; S. 14, Z. 20 live a life; S. 17, Z. 36 hither für hether; S. 27 Shakspere für Shakespere.

Litteratur.

The Works of Alfred Lord Tennyson, Poet Laureate. Macmillan & Co., London 1893.

The English Bible.

Cruden's Concordance to the English Bible, edited by Eadie. Griffin & Co., London.

Shaksperian Grammar von E. A. Abbott, Macmillan & Co., London.

Shakspere Lexicon von Alex. Schmidt, Williams & Norgate, London.

Chaucer, Prologue, the Knightes Tale etc. edited by Morris & Skeat. Clarendon Press, Oxford.

Spenser's Faery Queene, edited by Kitchen, Bks I und II. Clarendon Press.

Le Morte d'Arthur by Sir Thomas Malory. Original-Edition of William Caxton now reprinted by Dr. Sommer. Nutt, London 1891.

Mabinogian, collection of Welsh Tales translated into English by Lady Charlotte Guest. Longman 1838 London.

Vita.

Natus sum Georgus Thistlethwaite in oppido Ingleton pridie Kal. Jun. h. s. LVI, patre Eduardo, matre Elizabethe, e gente Parker. Fidei addictus sum evangelicae. Litterarum elementis imbutus in gymnasio Giggleswickiensi Londinii in tentamine matriculationis, quam dicimus, maturus iudicatus sum. Iamque per complures annos in litteras incubueram et in urbe Ma: /hester (civis universitatis Victoriensis) et Londinii (socius collegii universitatis), cum oculorum inflammatio, qua jam diu laborabam, tantopere increvit, ut litterarum studia intermittere et ad postremum omittere cogerer. Magister deinde fui gymnasii Batleyensis itemque docui pueros nobili loco natos, alumnos ludi Farnboroughensis. Insequenti tand anno medicus quidam ocularius, Germanus natione, morbum illum oculorum adeo depulerat, ut iterum scholas Londinenses adire unumque post annum gradum Baccalaurei Artium consequi possem. Docuerunt me viri doctissimi, London: Church, Croom Robertson, Goodwin, Cassal. — Manchester: Greenwood, Wilkins, Adamson, Ward, Toller.

Anno LXXXIX in Germaniam profectus primum per aestatem scholis professorum Heidelbergensium (Braune et Ihne) deinde ab autumno eiusdem anni Berolinensium (Er. Schmidt, Tobler, Weinhold, Zupitza) adfui. Vere anni XCIII. Halis Saxonum lector factus sum linguae Anglicae, quo munere adhuc fungor, adjutus comitate et benignitate cum aliorum tum professorum Wagner et Suchier, quorum utrique maximam me debere gratiam profiteri non dubito.